Modern Language Association of America

Approaches to Teaching World Literature

Joseph Gibaldi, Series Editor

1. Joseph Gibaldi, ed. *Approaches to Teaching Chaucer's* Canterbury Tales. 1980.
2. Carole Slade, ed. *Approaches to Teaching Dante's* Divine Comedy. 1982.
3. Richard Bjornson, ed. *Approaches to Teaching Cervantes'* Don Quixote. 1984.
4. Jess B. Bessinger, Jr., and Robert F. Yeager, eds. *Approaches to Teaching* Beowulf. 1984.
5. Richard J. Dunn, ed. *Approaches to Teaching Dickens'* David Copperfield. 1984.
6. Steven G. Kellman, ed. *Approaches to Teaching Camus's* The Plague. 1985.
7. Yvonne Shafer, ed. *Approaches to Teaching Ibsen's* A Doll House. 1985.
8. Martin Bickman, ed. *Approaches to Teaching Melville's* Moby-Dick. 1985.
9. Miriam Youngerman Miller and Jane Chance, eds. *Approaches to Teaching* Sir Gawain and the Green Knight. 1986.
10. Galbraith M. Crump, ed. *Approaches to Teaching Milton's* Paradise Lost. 1986.
11. Spencer Hall, with Jonathan Ramsey, eds. *Approaches to Teaching Wordsworth's Poetry.* 1986.
12. Robert H. Ray, ed. *Approaches to Teaching Shakespeare's* King Lear. 1986.
13. Kostas Myrsiades, ed. *Approaches to Teaching Homer's* Iliad *and* Odyssey. 1987.
14. Douglas J. McMillan, ed. *Approaches to Teaching Goethe's* Faust. 1987.
15. Renée Waldinger, ed. *Approaches to Teaching Voltaire's* Candide. 1987.
16. Bernard Koloski, ed. *Approaches to Teaching Chopin's* The Awakening. 1988.
17. Kenneth M. Roemer, ed. *Approaches to Teaching Momaday's* The Way to Rainy Mountain. 1988.
18. Edward J. Rielly, ed. *Approaches to Teaching Swift's* Gulliver's Travels. 1988.
19. Jewel Spears Brooker, ed. *Approaches to Teaching Eliot's Poetry and Plays.* 1988.
20. Melvyn New, ed. *Approaches to Teaching Sterne's* Tristram Shandy. 1989.
21. Robert F. Gleckner and Mark L. Greenberg, eds. *Approaches to Teaching Blake's* Songs of Innocence and of Experience. 1989.
22. Susan J. Rosowski, ed. *Approaches to Teaching Cather's* My Ántonia. 1989.
23. Carey Kaplan and Ellen Cronan Rose, eds. *Approaches to Teaching Lessing's* The Golden Notebook. 1989.

Approaches to Teaching Lessing's
The Golden Notebook

Edited by

Carey Kaplan &
Ellen Cronan Rose

The Modern Language Association of America
New York   1989

Library of Congress Cataloging-in-Publication Data

Approaches to teaching Lessing's The golden notebook / edited by Carey
   Kaplan and Ellen Cronan Rose.
      p.   cm. — (Approaches to teaching world literature ; 23)
   Bibliography: p.
   Includes index.
   ISBN 0-87352-521-3   ISBN 0-87352-522-1 (pbk.)
   1. Lessing, Doris May, 1919–   Golden notebook. 2. Lessing, Doris
May, 1919–   —Study and teaching. I. Kaplan, Carey. II. Rose,
Ellen Cronan, 1938– . III. Series.
PR6023.E833G633   1989
823'.914—dc19   88-30485

Cover illustration of the paperback edition: Joseph D'Addetta, "Eight Buddhist
Symbols," *Treasury of Chinese Design Motifs* (New York: Dover, 1981), 67.

Published by The Modern Language Association of America
10 Astor Place, New York, NY 10003-6981

CONTENTS

PREFACE TO THE SERIES

In *The Art of Teaching* Gilbert Highet wrote, "Bad teaching wastes a great deal of effort, and spoils many lives which might have been full of energy and happiness." All too many teachers have failed in their work, Highet argued, simply "because they have not thought about it." We hope that the Approaches to Teaching World Literature series, sponsored by the Modern Language Association's Committee on Teaching and Related Professional Activities, will not only improve the craft—as well as the art—of teaching but also encourage serious and continuing discussion of the aims and methods of teaching literature.

The principal objective of the series is to collect within each volume different points of view on teaching a specific literary work, a literary tradition, or a writer widely taught at the undergraduate level. The preparation of each volume begins with a wide-ranging survey of instructors, thus enabling us to include in the volume the philosophies and approaches, thoughts and methods of scores of experienced teachers. The result is a sourcebook of material, information, and ideas on teaching the subject of the volume to undergraduates.

The series is intended to serve nonspecialists as well as specialists, inexperienced as well as experienced teachers, graduate students who wish to learn effective ways of teaching as well as senior professors who wish to compare their own approaches with the approaches of colleagues in other schools. Of course, no volume in the series can ever substitute for erudition, intelligence, creativity, and sensitivity in teaching. We hope merely that each book will point readers in useful directions; at most each will offer only a first step in the long journey to successful teaching.

Joseph Gibaldi
Series Editor

INTRODUCTION

Early in *The Golden Notebook* Anna Wulf engages in an irritable dialogue with her friend and alter ego Molly, who cannot understand why Anna is writing eccentric, personal journals rather than novels.

> "What's in those diaries, then?" [Molly asks.]
> "They aren't diaries."
> "Whatever they are."
> "Chaos, that's the point." (41)

Throughout this thematically and structurally complex novel, Doris Lessing repeatedly invites the reader to contemplate the fragmentation of modern life through the mirroring lens of her fractured, intentionally chaotic and challenging work. Lessing insists that we grapple with the conflicting elements of her book in order to see the world anew. Refusal either of the writer, represented in the novel by its protagonist, Anna Wulf, or of the reader to meet this challenge results in personal diminishment or death. Because of Lessing's strong intellectual and moral conviction, *The Golden Notebook* has become a much studied touchstone of modern Western literature.

The Golden Notebook, though, is merely the centerpiece in an astonishing oeuvre. Since the publication of her first novel, *The Grass Is Singing*, in 1950, Lessing has published approximately thirty-five other works. Although she is best known for her novels, she has published several collections of stories, a few plays, a volume of poems, books of essays, and even some uncharacteristically fey jeux d'esprit, like *Particularly Cats*. She has published under the pseudonym Jane Somers as well as in her own name. Though primarily a realist, she has made significant excursions into fantasy and space fiction. There is also a large body of uncollected work: juvenilia, articles, essays, stories, and interviews.

Although *The Golden Notebook* is her most famous work, most of her other books receive continued recognition, which they well deserve, in North America and England, in most of the Commonwealth countries, and in Europe, Africa, and Asia. Lessing's books have been translated into Norwegian, Swedish, Danish, Italian, Belgian, French, German, Portuguese, Spanish, Japanese, Czechoslovakian, Russian, Dutch, Hungarian, Polish, Rumanian, Latvian, Arabic, and Finnish.

The Grass Is Singing was a runaway best-seller, the prototype of Anna

1

Wulf's ambivalently viewed *Frontiers of War* in *The Golden Notebook*. Lessing may feel about her first novel, a bleak, compelling, and still powerful meditation on apartheid's social and psychological consequences, what Anna Wulf feels for hers, that it is full of "lying nostalgia." Nonetheless, *The Grass Is Singing* established Lessing's reputation. The year following its publication, Lessing published a volume of African stories, many of which she probably wrote before the novel. This volume of stories, entitled *This Was the Old Chief's Country*, provides excellent background for the student interested in the African material in *The Golden Notebook*. In 1952 she began publishing the *Children of Violence* quintet with *Martha Quest*, a straightforward bildungsroman. *A Proper Marriage* followed in 1954. The *Children of Violence* series was then interrupted while Lessing wrote her now disowned novel *Retreat to Innocence* (1956); the profoundly moving recollection of her first return to Rhodesia since 1945, *Going Home* (1957); and another collection of stories—some African, most set in London—*The Habit of Loving* (1957). This hiatus may account for the different tone of the third *Children of Violence* novel, *A Ripple from the Storm* (1958). The most relentlessly political of her novels, it provides a significant gloss to the political aspects of *The Golden Notebook*.

Before the remarkable achievement of *The Golden Notebook*, Lessing published some (for her) relatively lightweight work: two plays, a volume of poetry, and a slight autobiographical narrative, *In Pursuit of the English* (1960). One of the dramas, *Play with a Tiger*, is a preliminary effort to deal with some of the Saul Green material in *The Golden Notebook*.

Then, in 1962, *The Golden Notebook* appeared. Although it was simultaneously published in England and the United States, it was not immediately acclaimed in either country. The novel's reputation grew slowly, not reaching its present eminence until the seventies.

In the meantime, Lessing brought out another volume of stories, *A Man and Two Women* (1963); *Landlocked* (1965), the fourth *Children of Violence* novel; and *Particularly Cats* (1967).

The Four-Gated City, the massive and magisterial final volume of *Children of Violence*, which appeared in 1969, marked new directions that would dominate Lessing's work for more than a decade: an apocalyptic vision; fascination with Jungian and Laingian psychologies in their most extreme manifestations; experimentation with stream-of-consciousness and space fiction; and a near obsession with Sufi philosophy. Lessing's most intimate exploration of Jungian-Laingian notions about madness, *Briefing for a Descent into Hell*, came out in 1971. *The Temptation of Jack Orkney and Other Stories* was published in 1972, followed by two plays and *The Summer before the Dark*, all in 1973.

The Memoirs of a Survivor (1974) is a short novel about the simultaneous breakdown of society and conventional reality in a futuristic, polluted, wrecked London. In the same year, Paul Schlueter edited a collection of interviews with and essays by Lessing, *A Small Personal Voice*, that gave her increasing body of readers tantalizing glimpses behind the mounting wall of fiction.

In 1979 Lessing distressed and confused some of her fans, especially American feminists who admired *The Golden Notebook* for its unflinching and relentless depiction of mid-twentieth-century women's lives, by stepping into outer space with the first of the *Canopus in Argos: Archives* novels, *Shikasta*. The others, mapping a massive intergalactic empire, followed rapidly: *The Marriages between Zones Three, Four and Five* (1980); *The Sirian Experiments* (1981); *The Making of the Representative for Planet 8* (1982); and *Documents Relating to the Sentimental Agents in the Volyen Empire* (1982).

Although such rapid writing astonished dedicated Lessing followers, she turned out to be even more prolific than supposed. While writing her space fiction, she had secretly returned to realism and written two books under the pseudonym Jane Somers, both centering on the general theme of aging: *The Diary of a Good Neighbor* (1983) and *If the Old Could . . .* (1984). When the hoax was unveiled, Lessing informed curious interviewers that the use of a nom de plume was meant to expose inequities in the corrupt world of publishing. Scholars and critics, of course, speculate about the metasignificance of this authorial fracture, so reminiscent of the complexities of the author of *The Golden Notebook*, in which Doris Lessing writes about Anna Wulf who writes about Anna Wulf who writes about Ella who writes about a suicidal young man.

In 1985 Lessing published a curiously irritable realistic novel, *The Good Terrorist*, and in 1988 *The Fifth Child*, a haunting semigothic novel about an evil child born into an ordinary middle-class family.

Perhaps none of her books, except *The Four-Gated City*, is as ambitious, comprehensive, and prescient as *The Golden Notebook*, but Doris Lessing's body of work, both in quantity and quality, is almost numbingly impressive. It is a stunning life's work, and almost at its center is the glowing and alluring gem, *The Golden Notebook*. Since its initial publication in 1962, *The Golden Notebook* has haunted, first, the common reader, then, increasingly in the past fifteen years, the academic critic, the pedagogue, and the curious but often mystified college student with its challenge to understanding and its impetus to re-vision.

For many students, *The Golden Notebook* is their only classroom exposure to Doris Lessing's writing because the work is widely recognized as offering the fullest statement of Lessing's philosophy and worldview in the most formally demanding matrix. The rare exceptions may be a short story or two in an introductory literature course; a quick reading of *Martha Quest* or *A*

Proper Marriage in a women's studies course; or one of the space fictions in a science fiction or popular literature course. Such exceptions do not begin to introduce the young reader to the rich, multifaceted, unflinching examination of the first half of the twentieth century that is Lessing's unique achievement in *The Golden Notebook*. Because it is Lessing's best known, most read, and most analyzed work, the book for which she is suggested again and again for the Nobel Prize in literature, her claim to have written a masterpiece and landmark of modern literature, *The Golden Notebook* deserves strong and comprehensive pedagogy.

The novel's structure is deliberately elaborate, reflecting its varied content that comprises, among other things, leftist politics before Stalin's death; trends in psychoanalysis; war and its effects on nations and individuals; speculation on art, writing, and the future of fiction; the whole gamut of male-female relations; and a Laingian-Jungian glimpse into the world of madness. Such variety obviously attracts a wide range of critical and pedagogical approaches, for this is a novel whose theme and structure insist that reality is chaotic, fragmentary, and resistant to any single interpretation. Given this complexity, we invited contributors to this *Approaches* volume to be as wide-ranging as possible in their suggestions and applications. The result is a rich mélange, composed of political history, literary history, critical theory, personal experience, and practical exercises.

One of the many reasons that we looked for such a variety of approaches, particularly political and historical, is that Lessing's characters work out their lives against an intricate tapestry of modern African and European events, frequently unfamiliar to students and difficult to find in any single text. Thus, while articles in this volume analyze the challenging structure of *The Golden Notebook*, we have also acknowledged the novel's passionate engagement in the historical moment. *The Golden Notebook*, resolutely rejecting the stylistic pyrotechnics characteristic of modernist and postmodernist fiction, is full of diaries, memoirs, personal archival records, letters, notebooks, news clippings, and rough drafts. The material, moreover, is notoriously autobiographical, blurring the line between writer and work of fiction already confusing to most students. Even when Lessing treats intellectual notions, political ideology, or cosmic teleology, her tone is deeply personal. Long before the women's movement enunciated the dictum "The personal is political," Lessing's work demonstrated the point repeatedly and forcefully.

Furthermore, multiple approaches are entirely in keeping with Lessing's own sense of her novel. Indeed, in her preface to *The Golden Notebook*, she implores that the work not be treated reductively, that it not be neatly pigeonholed into a pedagogical, interpretive, or ideological slot. Lessing emphasized this caveat on 25 April 1984 when, appearing on the popular nightly news program, National Public Radio's *All Things Considered*, she retorted testily to Susan Stamberg's question about whether she wrote "to show us the world as it is, or the world as it should be, or the world as it might be": "Why do you make it 'or, or, or'? It could be 'and, and, and.' " Later she returned to this point, suggesting that "either/or" has "very little to do with how things really are. . . . Because, you know, that's how the computer works. They call it the binary mode, don't they? The *this* or *that*, the switch. This or that. I'm asking myself, is the computer, the way it functions, a model of the human mind?" ("Interview," with Stamberg, 4).

In compiling this volume, then, we have tried to offer a representative selection of ways of looking at, talking about, and teaching Lessing. The responses to our initial questionnaire indicated the variety of applications we should include. *The Golden Notebook*, we learned from our respondents, was taught on undergraduate and graduate levels; in women's studies classes ranging from introductory courses to advanced graduate seminars; in intro- duction-to-fiction courses; in graduate courses on the contemporary British novel and on the psychological novel, among other topics; in courses on major authors at all levels; in graduate courses on literary theory; in creative writing courses; in Commonwealth literature courses; in politics and liter- ature courses; in seminars on both modernism and postmodernism; in one course dauntingly and imperially entitled The Contemporary World; and even in film courses because of its filmic archetype, the projectionist.

The people teaching these courses asked for an Approaches volume that would include background information extending from the history of fem- inism to the history of Marxism; from the history of fiction to the sociology of women and ethnic minorities. They requested essays on Commonwealth literature; world literature, especially African; Jungian and Freudian psy- choanalysis and philosophy; and the impact of world wars I and II on Eu- ropean culture and history. Gratifyingly, some respondents were eager to write the very essays others wanted.

To all who responded to our questionnaire, we are grateful for the thought- ful comments and suggestions that provided the basis for part 1 of this book, "Materials." This section recommends background reading to supplement the essays in part 2 and surveys and evaluates for its pedagogical utility the potentially overwhelming corpus of scholarly and critical material published on *The Golden Notebook* in the last twenty-five years.

Part 2 of the book, "Approaches," was written by teachers of *The Golden Notebook* and is arranged in three comprehensive categories: background information useful for placing the novel historically, politically, philosophi- cally, and aesthetically; pragmatic discussions on teaching the novel in a wide variety of times, circumstances, and classrooms; and more speculative and theoretical essays that suggest, without specifying, new applications in the classroom. The contributors teach at colleges and universities all over the United States, Canada, and South Africa and vary widely in age, experience, and critical orientation. All are united by compelling personal and pedagogical interest in Doris Lessing's elusive, allusive, demanding masterwork.

The "Backgrounds" section begins with Dee Seligman's biographical essay, "In Pursuit of Doris Lessing," especially valuable because no single book or essay presents the available information about Lessing. Seligman's interest in the autobiographical aspect of Lessing's writings has resulted in a useful collation of facts about the author's life with their correlatives in *The Golden Notebook* and other works.

As important to a reading of *The Golden Notebook* as Lessing's life is the African historical context. Eve Bertelsen's piece emphasizes how Lessing was affected by such movements and events as Rhodesian partition, race relations, the Labor movement, and Communist party activity in the colony, especially during World War II.

Frederick Stern's essay on politics in the mid-fifties is particularly useful for contemporary students. Stern elucidates such mysteries as leftist factionalism, the Stalinist schism, and the effects of McCarthyism and the cold war, both in the United States and Europe.

Jean Pickering explores the principal philosophical currents in *The Golden Notebook*. Her essay describes and explains such influences on Lessing as Jungian and Freudian psychoanalysis; the "antipsychiatry" of R. D. Laing; existentialism, especially as exemplified by Camus and Beauvoir; and the socialist-realist aesthetics of Marxism and Leninism.

No single twentieth-century thinker has had more effect on the structure and meaning of *The Golden Notebook* than Carl Jung. Lorelei Cederstrom's essay, "The Principal Archetypal Elements of *The Golden Notebook*," explains and illuminates this important influence on Lessing's intellectual and artistic life.

Marjorie Lightfoot productively plays *The Golden Notebook* off against *The Waste Land* and *Ulysses*. Her essay highlights the angst, anomie, and temptation to nihilism that plague both modernist and postmodernist authors.

In the first essay in the "Spectrum of Classrooms" section Joseph Hynes, who has taught *The Golden Notebook* since the early sixties in a two-semester graduate seminar on contemporary British fiction, discusses changing attitudes toward it over the years and strategies for keeping it from becoming an archaic cultural artifact. Roberta Rubenstein explains the problems and challenges inherent in teaching *The Golden Notebook* in a broad-based introductory women's studies course that includes units on the history, sociology, and philosophy of feminism and addresses non-English majors with little "experience as readers of imaginative narrative." Claire Sprague describes inserting Lessing into F. R. Leavis's Great Tradition in a course on George Eliot and Doris Lessing. The analogies and contrasts she develops and exploits point in particularly fruitful directions for instructors teaching courses such as major British authors. By contrast, Molly Hite, a young professor at Cornell, describes teaching *The Golden Notebook* in the context of a graduate seminar emphasizing experimental, postmodernist fiction and using current literary theory. Equally specialized and at the same time broadly suggestive is Ruth Saxton's innovative methodology for teaching *The Golden Notebook* to students primarily interested in creative writing. Her premise that imitation of style, technique, and structure helps develop critical and analytical ability may be applicable in numerous classrooms.

Section three, "Pedagogical Challenges and Opportunities," indicates ways in which *The Golden Notebook* can be illuminatingly integrated into various critical and theoretical constructs. Sharon Hileman, eager to involve uninitiated undergraduates, suggests strategies for lectures, in- and out-of-class writing assignments, questions, and even quizzes. *The Golden Notebook* is a keystone in Virginia Tiger's graduate seminar Autobiographical Encodings, which includes such texts as Rousseau's *Confessions*, Woolf's *To the Lighthouse*, and Anaïs Nin's *Diaries*. Mona Knapp describes methods of using the novel to define feminist literary criticism(s). Sharon R. Wilson inventively incorporates film theory as a way of opening the novel to students more familiar with the visual than the verbal. Similarly, Sandra Brown's "*The Golden Notebook* as Fugue" looks to musical form for an evocative reading of the work. Finally, to end where Lessing might have us begin, Katherine Fishburn, in "*The Golden Notebook*: A Challenge to the Teaching Establishment," takes to heart Lessing's advice to readers in her preface to the novel that they "read the book on their own without any form of outside interference." Fishburn teaches the novel, but always with a wary eye on its writer's mistrust of the pedagogical endeavor.

Carey Kaplan and
Ellen Cronan Rose

Part One

MATERIALS

*Carey Kaplan &
Ellen Cronan Rose*

Text

Since all currently available editions of *The Golden Notebook* are prefaced by Lessing's 1971 "introduction," the choice of which text to assign—to graduates or undergraduates, English majors or nonmajors, students at two-year colleges or university students—is purely financial. While doctoral candidates and professors might be willing to pay five times more for a durable, hardcover edition of the text, undergraduates who buy the Bantam paperback will read essentially the same *Golden Notebook* as the more affluent. "Essentially" but not pragmatically, since the pagination in the Bantam paperback is different from that in the Simon and Schuster hardcover edition. We have, therefore, conceded to the interest of the majority and refer, throughout this book, to the Bantam edition.

Background

Irving Howe, one of the earliest and most astute readers of *The Golden Notebook*, claimed that its "particular distinction" arose from Doris Lessing's understanding that "personal relations" are inextricably embedded in and affected by larger historical forces (17). The specific historical forces acting on Anna Wulf are explored at some length in essays in this volume by Eve Bertelsen, Jean Pickering, Frederick Stern, and Mona Knapp, while Dee Seligman has provided information about Lessing which suggests that much of Anna's "personal" sensibility is determined by her creator's experience. Some instructors may, however, want to supplement these essays with additional reading.

Though Lessing has discouraged would-be biographers, she has left a tantalizing spoor for them to follow in autobiographical works such as *Going Home*, *Particularly Cats*, "My Father," "Being Prohibited," and "The Fruits of Humbug" (three essays reprinted in *A Small Personal Voice*), and two essays about her mother published in *Granta*, "Autobiography: Impertinent Daughters" and "Autobiography (Part Two): My Mother's Life." Supplementing these are numerous interviews she has granted over the years. Of particular interest to readers of *The Golden Notebook* are her interviews with Roy Newquist, Florence Howe, and Jonah Raskin, conveniently republished in *A Small Personal Voice*. For the insatiably curious, the bibliography in Eve Bertelsen's *Doris Lessing* lists twenty-three additional interviews, from 1962 to 1984. Bertelsen's deconstruction of her own interview with Lessing (in Kaplan and Rose) should, however, caution the curious against accepting Lessing's self-portrait uncritically, as should Virginia Tiger's essay in this book. As Dee Seligman suggests, we do better to "tease out" the facts of Lessing's life from a variety of sources, including people who knew her. Seligman herself interviewed a number of Lessing's Rhodesian acquaintances, including her brother Harry Tayler; she has recorded her discoveries in "The Four-Faced Novelist."

Bertelsen's essay in this volume on the Rhodesian background of *The Golden Notebook* is usefully augmented by her 1985 collection of essays, *Doris Lessing*. It includes Murray Steele's "Doris Lessing's Rhodesia," Anthony Chennells's "Doris Lessing and the Rhodesian Settler Novel," and Jenny Taylor's "Memory and Desire on Going Home: The Deconstruction of a Colonial Radical," in addition to Bertelsen's long, probing interview with Lessing. (Bertelsen's *Doris Lessing* is not distributed in this country.)

Additional materials that will enhance the instructor's appreciation of African elements in *The Golden Notebook* include James Barber's *Rhodesia: The Road to Rebellion*, Anthony Beck's "Doris Lessing and the Colonial Experience," Robert Blake's *History of Rhodesia*, Richard Gray's *Two Nations: Aspects of the Development of Race Relations in the Rhodesias and Nyasaland*, Martin Loney's *Rhodesia: White Racism and Imperial Response*, Terence Ranger's *African Voice in Southern Rhodesia (1898–1930)* and *Aspects of Central African History*, Murray Steele's "White Working Class Disunity: The Southern Rhodesia Labour Party," Lawrence Vambe's *Ill-Fated People: Rhodesia before and after Rhodes*, and A. K. H. Weinrich's *Black and White Elites in Rural Rhodesia*.

The Golden Notebook also reflects the troubled "situation of women" analyzed by Simone de Beauvoir in *The Second Sex* and named, finally, by Betty Friedan in *The Feminine Mystique* as "the problem that has no name" which produced the feminist movement of the late sixties and the seventies. Instructors teaching the novel to today's "postfeminist" generation will benefit from consulting not only the historical documents of the women's movement cited in Mona Knapp's essay but also Karen Ray's "Ethics of Feminism in the Literature Classroom: A Delicate Balance" and Hoyt Gimlin's collection of essays *The Women's Movement: Agenda for the '80s*. The instructor will also find ideas for relating *The Golden Notebook* to feminist history and theory in Elaine Showalter's *New Feminist Criticism: Essays on Women, Literature and Theory* and Judith Newton and Deborah Rosenfelt's *Feminist Criticism and Social Change*.

Scholars who, unlike Frederick Stern, are not fluent in German will be glad to know that Hugo Dewar's article on the Communist party in Britain in *Die Kommunistischen Parteien der Welt* is not the only source of information about leftist and Communist history relevant to *The Golden Note-*

book. Valuable information on the climate Stern describes in his "Backgrounds" essay appears in Giuseppa Boffa's *Inside the Khrushchev Era,* Theodore Draper's *Roots of American Communism,* Vivian Gornick's *Romance of American Communism,* Eric J. Hobsbawm's *Revolutionaries,* Leszek Kolakowski's *Main Currents of Marxism: Its Rise, Growth and Desolation,* Albert S. Lindeman's *History of European Socialism,* Keith Middlemas's *Power and the Party: Changing Forces of Communism in Western Europe,* Jean-Paul Sartre's *Specter of Stalin,* Alan Sked and Chris Cook's *Post-War Britain: A Political History,* and Paolo Spriano's *Stalin and the European Communists.*

Books like these amplify the sketch Stern has drawn of the ideological climate of the Left in the fifties, but they do not directly explain why the theme of the artist's relation to society that threads through *The Golden Notebook* is intertwined with the theme of Anna's relation to the Communist party or why, in the midst of a lecture on Socialist art (350), Anna stammers, unable to finish.

To answer these questions, instructors need to familiarize themselves with attitudes about art and about the role of the artist that prevailed in leftist and Marxist circles in the years following World War II. Lessing's essay "The Small Personal Voice" (1957) is indispensable, but it should be supplemented by Jack Lindsay's *After the "Thirties,"* Jean-Paul Sartre's *What Is Literature?*, Georg Lukács's *Meaning of Contemporary Realism,* and Raymond Williams's *Long Revolution.*

Lessing Criticism

When *The Golden Notebook* was published in 1962, it attracted the attention of "serious" journalist-critics like Irving Howe, Orville Prescott, and Granville Hicks. But even though they claimed that *The Golden Notebook* was "the most exciting piece of new fiction" produced in the decade (Howe 20), they couldn't have foreseen that by 1985 scholarly interest in Doris Lessing would have generated seventeen books, fifty-nine doctoral dissertations, and over three hundred articles. From this daunting critical corpus, how is the instructor to know what is helpful, if not essential, to teaching *The Golden Notebook* responsibly?

Dee Seligman's invaluable *Doris Lessing: An Annotated Bibliography of Criticism* is the place to start, but it is only a start, since Seligman stopped annotating (and compiling) Lessing criticism in 1978. The most comprehensive bibliography since Seligman's is contained in the concluding twenty-two pages of Eve Bertelsen's *Doris Lessing,* but as it is not annotated, we will attempt to identify here the outstanding approaches to *The Golden Notebook* from a variety of critical perspectives.

Nine years after its first publication, infuriated by critics and reviewers who insisted on reading *The Golden Notebook* as "a tract about the sex war" (*GN* x), Doris Lessing wrote a preface to the novel (included as an "introduction" in the Bantam edition) in which she imperially established the interpretive parameters by which she meant her novel to be read. The "themes" she identified were psychological, historical-political, and aesthetic: breakdown or "madness" as a path to psychic health, the ideological "feel" of the fifties, and the artist as exemplary hero. At the same time that she was writing "a novel of ideas," however, her "major aim was to shape a book which would make its own comment, a wordless statement: to talk through the way it was shaped" (*GN* xiv).

By and large, since 1971 academic criticism of *The Golden Notebook* has dutifully pursued the hermeneutic hints embedded in Lessing's introduction. We say "by and large" because, dismissing as naive Lessing's assumption that "the filter which is a woman's way of looking at life" is essentially no different from "the filter which is a man's way" (*GN* xi), feminist critics have appropriated *The Golden Notebook* for their increasingly sophisticated projects of representing women's experience authentically, reformulating the canon, and revising narrative theory.

Published criticism of *The Golden Notebook* falls into three categories. Two of them—psychological and formal—correspond roughly to the themes Lessing announces in her preface, while the third category—feminist criticism—stoutly ignores it. There has been appallingly little historical-political—that is, Marxist—criticism of *The Golden Notebook*; Jenny Taylor's anthology, *Notebooks/Memoirs/Archives: Reading and Rereading Doris Lessing*, is an auspicious exception.

Taking their cue from Lessing, who gives Anna Wulf a Jungian analyst, a number of critics have brought, with varying degrees of rigor or flexibility, a Jungian perspective to bear on the interrelated themes of "breakdown" and the exemplary heroism of the artist. Representative and especially useful are Lorelei Cederstrom's "Process of Individuation in *The Golden Notebook*," Annis Pratt's "Contrary Structure of Doris Lessing's *The Golden Notebook*," Evelyn J. Hinz and John J. Teunissen's "Pieta as Icon in *The Golden Notebook*," and the *Golden Notebook* chapters in Mary Ann Singleton's *City and the Veld: The Fiction of Doris Lessing* and in Roberta Rubenstein's *Novelistic Vision of Doris Lessing: Breaking the Forms of Consciousness*.

These and other critics also discuss Anna's "madness" in the interior "Golden Notebook" as an example of R. D. Laing's theory that "schizophrenia is a natural process of mind-healing which, if allowed to run its full course, will be therapeutic rather than destructive" (Rubenstein, *Novelistic Vision* 179). The classic essays here are Marion Vlastos's "Doris Lessing and R. D. Laing:

Psychopolitics and Prophecy" and Roberta Rubenstein's "Briefing on Inner
Space: Doris Lessing and R. D. Laing." Phyllis Sternberg Perrakis uses
Nancy Chodorow's theory of "boundary confusion" to account for Anna's
debilitating dependency on surrogate mothers (often male) in "Doris Lessing's *Golden Notebook*: Separation and Symbiosis."

While psychological critics tend to focus on Anna's madness or on archetypal patterning in the novel, feminists concentrate on trying to define the
peculiarly female dimensions of Anna's psychic and creative makeup. There
are extended discussions of *The Golden Notebook* in such classics of feminist
criticism as Patricia Meyer Spacks's *Female Imagination*, Sydney Janet Kaplan's *Feminine Consciousness in the Modern British Novel*, and Elaine Showalter's *Literature of Their Own*. Until very recently, feminist criticism of
The Golden Notebook has been of the "images of women" variety. Note-
worthy examples include Ellen Brooks's "Image of Women in Lessing's *The
Golden Notebook*," Ellen Morgan's "Alienation of the Woman Writer in *The
Golden Notebook*," Lynn Sukenick's "Feeling and Reason in Doris Lessing's
Fiction," Sharon Spencer's "Femininity and the Woman Writer: Doris Les-
sing's *The Golden Notebook* and the *Diary* of Anaïs Nin," Marion Vlastos
Libby's "Sex and the New Woman in *The Golden Notebook*," Alice Bradley
Markow's "Pathology of Feminine Failure in the Fiction of Doris Lessing,"
and Elayne Antler Rapping's "Unfree Women: Feminism in Doris Lessing's
Novels." In the past few years, however, feminist critics interested in narrative theory have returned to *The Golden Notebook* with fresh insights.
Outstanding and provocative are Elizabeth Abel's "*Golden Notebook*: 'Female Writing' and 'The Great Tradition,' " Patrocinio Schweickart's "Reading
a Wordless Statement: The Structure of Doris Lessing's *The Golden Notebook*," and a few highly suggestive pages (101–04) on *The Golden Notebook*
in Rachel Blau DuPlessis's *Writing beyond the Ending: Narrative Strategies
of Twentieth-Century Women Writers*.

In these recent essays, feminist critics significantly modify a formalist strain
of Lessing criticism that has prevailed since 1973, when Joseph Hynes's
"Construction of *The Golden Notebook*" and John L. Carey's "Art and Reality
in *The Golden Notebook*" revolutionized our way of reading the novel and
spawned a number of what might loosely be called structural readings of
The Golden Notebook, emphasizing its metafictional, self-reflexive qualities.
A number of critics since then have delicately unpacked this Chinese box
of a novel, many of them in the spirit Joseph Hynes expressed when he
concluded his article with the hope that his "structural and aesthetic" over-
view of the novel would be a prolegomenon to interpretation. Hynes's and
Carey's articles are indispensable reading for the instructor; additional help
in discerning and teaching the novel's structure will be found in Anne Mulkeen's "Twentieth-Century Realism: The 'Grid' Structure of *The Golden*

Notebook," Martha Lifson's "Structural Patterns in *The Golden Notebook*," Anne Hedin's "Mandala: Blueprint for Change in Lessing's Later Fiction," and Betsy Draine's "Nostalgia and Irony: The Postmodern Order of *The Golden Notebook*."

The Golden Notebook needs the most imaginative and innovative pedagogy we can devise, for as Lessing accurately insists in her preface, "the essence of the book, the organization of it, everything in it, says implicitly and explicitly, that we must not divide things off, must not compartmentalize" (x). The challenge to teachers is to resist their own and their students' desire for critical closure, zealously guarding against the oversimplified misreading that would result from slavishly applying any one approach to the novel. *The Golden Notebook* challenges us to come up with critical paradigms more comprehensive than any currently in fashion.

Lessing concluded her preface to *The Golden Notebook* by suggesting that a book is "alive and potent and fructifying and able to promote thought and discussion *only* when its plan and shape and intention are not understood, because that moment of seeing the shape and plan and intention is also the moment when there isn't anything more to be got out of it" (xxiv). We believe the approaches to teaching *The Golden Notebook* represented in this volume will open rather than close debate about this continually fascinating book, will provoke rather than resolve critical controversy, and will ensure that *The Golden Notebook* remains alive—and kicking—in classrooms for a long time.

Additional Resources

The *Doris Lessing Newsletter*, published twice a year, contains a wealth of material instructors will find useful: archival material such as letters Lessing wrote in 1956 to the Marxist publication the *Reasoner*, a continuously updated bibliography of Lessing criticism, reviews of books by and about Lessing, teaching suggestions, a forum where readers can exchange views, and short critical essays on Lessing's stories, plays, and poems, as well as her novels. Published by the Doris Lessing Society, an Allied Organization of the MLA, the *Doris Lessing Newsletter* can be found in many university libraries; a subscription to it is included with membership in the DLS, whose current president is listed in the Directory of Allied Organizations in each November's issue of *PMLA*.

Gerry Mulligan's "Golden Notebooks" is, unfortunately, out of print. But you don't have to haunt your neighborhood secondhand record dealer to locate a copy of Doris Lessing reading from *The Golden Notebook* and other works; it's available on Caedmon TC1753 and cassette CP1753.

Finally, and frivolously, if you are ever in Woodstock, New York, stop by the Golden Notebooks bookstore and pick up a handful of their bookmarks to indicate the serial appearance, in your Bantam *Golden Notebook*, of black 1, 2, 3, 4; red 1, 2, 3, 4; yellow 1, 2, 3, 4, and so on.

Part Two

APPROACHES

BACKGROUNDS

In Pursuit of Doris Lessing

Dee Seligman

Doris Lessing's uncanny ability to touch the pulse of the present derives from her ability to maintain a detached but observant perspective on her own life experiences. This biographical essay merely attempts to give a context for some of the themes and characters of *The Golden Notebook*. Lessing is opposed to a biographical approach to her works since critics have oversimplified the relationship between her characters and real people. Yet we do know that there is some correspondence between her life and her works. At best, this essay will "tease out" the facts of her life from interviews, biographical essays, and other works by people she knew.

Doris is the oldest child of Alfred Cook Tayler, called Michael by his wife and children, and Emily Maude McVeagh Tayler. Born in 1919 in Persia, Doris lived there the first five years of her life, during which time her younger brother, Harry Tayler, was also born. Her mother, a nurse, had worked in the London hospital where her father recuperated from shell shock and an amputated leg after serving in World War I. Living in Persia was a very happy time for her mother and a less happy time for her father, who had a banking job. Moody and disillusioned, Michael eventually returned the family to England, from which they emigrated to Southern Rhodesia, where he hoped to make a fortune as a maize farmer.

However, life in Rhodesia was not what they expected. The land was virgin bush, thick with small game, sparsely dotted with farms miles apart worked by Africans. The family settled on the rich red soil of a town called

Banket, where, struggling financially, they lived for twenty years in a ramshackle "pole and daga" (mud) house. Lessing's father lost a great deal of money when the price of maize dropped. Her mother led an emotionally isolated existence, while the two children roamed the bush, hunting and living in solitude. Their parents suffered many ailments, some caused by nerves, others by physical disabilities. In addition, there was much stress between Doris and Maude, who was ambitious for her daughter. Eventually Doris was sent, at seven, to a Catholic convent school in Salisbury. It proved harsh and oppressive; after six years she was withdrawn and enrolled in a government-run school for a year. At fourteen, rejecting formal schooling, she continued to educate herself by omnivorous reading. At sixteen she became a Salisbury telephone operator, then wrote "two bad novels" while residing at her parents' farm. She married Frank Wisdom, a civil servant, in 1939 at age nineteen. The couple had two children, a son, John, and a daughter, Jean, during their four years of marriage. Memories from the farm years and first marriage color the *Children of Violence* series, *Going Home*, and Lessing's African stories.

Chafing at the confinement of married life and the conservative political views of her circle of married friends, Lessing managed to meet some of the visiting members of the Royal Air Force who were training in Salisbury for the war. They represented both a progressive attitude toward world politics and the heady euphoric atmosphere of war. She began to attend the Current Affairs Group, part of a book-club movement known in England as the Left Book Club, heavily influenced by the Communist party and claiming fifty thousand members worldwide (Sworakowski 165). She also joined the Rhodesian Friends of the Soviet Union, organized about May 1942. She subsequently joined a group that, frustrated with the Friends organization's weak impact, formed a Left Club, a collective modeled on the Communist party (Steele, "Doris Lessing's Rhodesia" 51). Membership in this group was as close to the Communist party as Doris actually came at this point. She describes the group as "so pure it must have been blessed by Lenin in his grave" (Lessing, "Witness"). This group, the only one committed to fighting the racism of Rhodesian culture and one sustained by the feverish energy of war, included the members of Parliament J. B. Lister and Donald McIntyre, as well as the political activists Nathan Zelter and Dorothy Zelter, RAF airmen, and European exiles, such as her second husband, Gottfried Lessing (Taylor, *Notebooks* 21). Lessing describes the experience:

> I was emotionally a communist in Rhodesia, where there was no communist party because the then legal system wouldn't have accommodated one. We created a highly romantic, idealistic, rather marvellous thing which had no connection at all with anything around us. ("Interview," with Ziegler and Bigsby, 196)

In 1945 she divorced Frank Wisdom and married Gottfried Anton Lessing, a half-Jewish German refugee and member of her "Communist" group, utterly different in culture and intellectual interests from her first husband. Together they had a son, Peter, born in 1947, when Doris was twenty-eight years old. By this time she had not only worked as a typist for two legal offices but had also worked as a specialized typist for *Hansard*, the official Parliamentary record. The Lessings became active in Marxist politics, working frenetically with their small group, believing all the while that "the whole world would be communist in about ten years' time, or it might take fifteen to create Utopia" (Bertelsen 107). After the war, the Lessings decided to divorce and to emigrate from Rhodesia. They left by way of Cape Town, South Africa, where Doris lived with her son Peter for a while, publishing poems and stories in South African journals. Her ex-husband continued to East Germany, where he remarried. Doris raised Peter in London, making her literary debut in 1950 with the publication of *The Grass Is Singing*.

In London, politically much more evolved than Rhodesia, the formal structures of communism had existed for some time and party members ran for office in Parliament. Lessing joined the Communist party in 1952. She says that she met most of the important people in the party but that she was never active as a party member, that she never went to meetings and did not know the "grass roots communist movement" (Bertelsen 116). Along with many other intellectuals she resigned in 1956 after Khrushchev's secret speech at the Twentieth Party Congress.

Before she left the party, Lessing became part of a group critical of party policy. In June 1956 a small mimeographed publication, the *Reasoner*, edited by Edward Thompson and John Saville, was first circulated in England. Its purpose was to bring about change from within. After three issues, the *Reasoner* was succeeded by the *New Reasoner*, still under Saville and Thompson's editorship, with Doris Lessing as one of four on the editorial board. One of her short stories appeared in an issue of this publication. Lessing acknowledges that her name was on the first issues but insists that Saville and Thompson merely used her flat in London for one or two meetings and that she never did any of the work (Bertelsen 116). Nevertheless she did remain on the editorial board until the publication of the November-December 1961 issue of the *New Left Review*, which was formed by the merger of *Reasoner* and the *Universities and Left Review*. In October 1956 she wrote a letter to the *New Reasoner* emphasizing the daily necessity of making fresh decisions "of just how much of our individual responsibility we are prepared to delegate to a central body—whether it is the communist party or the government of the country we live in." A month earlier she had written in an editorial in the *Reasoner* that criticism of the party should be done at a full party congress and that the job of intellectuals was to think and reexamine their position vis-à-vis the party, "not to have scapegoats, confessions, and breast-beating" (Sprague, "*Reasoner* Letters" 8, 7). Lessing cosigned a letter with E. P. Thompson, Rodney Hilton, Eric Hobsbawm, Christopher Hill, and others in the *New Statesman* and the *Tribune*, which condemned British party leadership and the Soviet invasion of Hungary (Taylor, *Notebooks* 26).

In the late fifties Lessing became an active member of the Committee for Nuclear Disarmament (CND), which organized the first Aldermaston March. She was one of the platform speakers on this historic march and participated in other antinuclear demonstrations. She continued to address issues of personal commitment and communism through the late fifties and early sixties in her novel *Retreat to Innocence* (1956), in her play *Each His Own Wilderness* (1958), and, of course, in *The Golden Notebook*. However, by 1961 she became ambivalent toward Socialists who live under the "darkening fog of urbane authoritarianism under which we caper and prance, getting our kicks from shouting insults at the police, thumbing our noses at wicked capitalists from the Royal Court stage, using irrelevant shibboleths like: Socialists must not criticise one another publicly" (Lessing, "Smart Set Socialists" 822).

Lessing's experience and reading were leading her into new territory. What she discovered in her studies was a long, circuitous path that led her from psychoanalysis with a Jungian therapist through an affair with the American expatriate writer Clancy Sigal to an interest in the politics of madness as represented by the British psychiatrist R. D. Laing to her eventual discovery of Islamic mysticism or Sufism.

Lessing at first was suspicious of Jungian views. For example, in 1961 she wrote a book review in which she satirized the heavy-handed use of Jungian archetypes to portray the Kalahari bushmen as embodiments of harmony and innocence (Taylor 22). However, Lessing describes her own Jungian therapist as "somewhat like Mrs. Marks":

> She was Roman Catholic, Jungian, and conservative. It was very upsetting to me at the time, but I found out it didn't matter a damn. I couldn't stand her terminology, but she was a marvelous person. She was one of those rare individuals who know how to help others. If she had used another set of words, if she had talked Freud talk, or aggressive atheism, it wouldn't have made a difference.   (Raskin 68)

Apparently this woman served as the friend Lessing needed in a troubled time.

Lessing acknowledges that she used Jungian notions and this "close work of the imagination" in dealing with her love life in her late thirties and early forties (roughly the late 1950s, during the time *The Golden Notebook* was probably being written) because her love life "was in a state of chaos and disarray and generally no good to me or to anybody else and I was, in fact, and I knew it, in a pretty bad way" ("Interview," with Ziegler and Bigsby, 203–04). Elsewhere she describes her life at that time as having an "intensity that I was living and writing" (Bertelsen 112). It is likely that Lessing here is referring to her affair with Clancy Sigal.

Sigal, a leftist, raised in the Labor movement and the Communist party, had served in the United States Army during World War II, completed his education after the war at the University of California, worked in Hollywood as a story analyst and agent, and then left the States in disgust and despair in the midst of Eisenhower apathy and conservatism. Sigal's first book, which gave him his following as a "cult author," was *Going Away*, published in 1962. It is a highly autobiographical "report and memoir," as he subtitles the novel, of America's "slide to conservatism" in the fifties set against the cross-country journey of an ex–Hollywood agent who travels east to New York looking up old friends along the way. It is a journey of despair, as he tries to establish continuity with his past political radicalism in a country that virtually ignored the Hungarian revolution and the subsequent Soviet repression. It reads as a harmonic and compelling counterpoint to the tone of *The Golden Notebook*.

Lessing's American readers informally accept Sigal as a probable source for *The Golden Notebook*'s Saul Green, since the identifying characteristics are so similar. Further tantalizing bits of evidence for this view come from a more recent novel by Sigal, *Zone of the Interior* (1976). He alludes frequently in this autobiographical fiction to a broken love affair with "Coral," a British woman writer; she had introduced him to Willie Last, who bears a striking resemblance to the Scots psychiatrist R. D. Laing. When Coral tired of the narrator Sid Bell's cold sweats, vertigo, and stomachaches and of his waking her up at three in the morning, she sent him off to Last (the symptoms sound very much like Saul's "breakdown" in *The Golden Notebook*). After their affair, Coral got Sid "out of her system" by writing a play about them, titled *Scorpions in a Bottle* (cf. Lessing's *Play with a Tiger*, in which Saul again appears with Anna), and Coral has also written a book in which Sid Bell figures as Paul, the American lover of Hannah in her novel *Loose Leaves from a Random Life* (cf. Saul and Anna in *The Golden Notebook*). Coral also sounds like Lessing because she is said to be developing a "rational mysticism in sessions with her Jungian shrink" and because her next novel is going to be about "how the world nearly ends and is saved by the mentally ill" (surely a reference to the end of *The Four-Gated City*).

Lessing admires R. D. Laing and in the past has described him as "very courageous . . . to question the basic assumptions of his profession from the inside" (Oates 875). More recently she has said that she has never idealized madness but that

> a great many people who are in mental hospitals should never have been there in the first place. It's not only I who think that, but a great many psychiatrists. There's now a way of looking at it—that madness is certainly often created by other people. That doesn't mean to say I think that there's no such thing as madness, of course there is. Cause if you've ever lived with anyone who's mad, you'll know there's nothing to be romantic about.   (Bertelsen 112)

Although Sigal has returned to the United States, their relationship and the acquaintance with Laing obviously deeply influenced Lessing. Whether she experienced the psychic breakdown that her character Anna did or whether she was merely a keen observer of what was happening to Sigal is difficult to ascertain.

Lessing's work moved on to some new concerns after *The Golden Notebook*, although all of it shares continuity with her earlier life. She still writes about the self but with the new perspective that "we [writers] are not unique and remarkable people," so that in writing truthfully about the self the writer is also writing about a lot of other people ("Interview," with Ziegler and Bigsby, 198).

Even though Lessing has little use for the academic enterprise, she believes strongly in the mind's resourcefulness. Since 1964 she has had a sustained interest in Islamic mysticism or Sufism. In that year she published her first review of a work by Idries Shah, *The Sufis*. Lessing admires Shah and frequently reviews his work, especially acknowledging the instructive force of Sufi parables and stories.

As promulgated by Shah, Sufism invites people to open the doors of perception. It promotes reaching one's full potential for the sake of the human race. While most of us depend on logic peppered with common sense as our guide, Sufism devalues logic. The Sufi teacher emphasizes deconditioning and the use of all the senses, including telepathy and higher psychic processes, to achieve full knowledge. Higher evolution of the species is the Sufi focus. Like the Zen teachers, Sufis use parables, ironic stories, music, and movement to help the learner. Integration of the self and reconciliation of opposites is the highest stage for the Sufi. As individuals progress to higher stages of evolution, Sufism suggests, the human race will move beyond the worldly perils of nationalism, political chicanery, and nuclear destruction.

Sufism as a body of literature might have been new to Lessing in the sixties, but it confirmed her own way of thinking, as she indicated in a series of lectures for the Canadian Broadcasting Corporation, published as *Prisons*

We Choose to Live In (1987). In these talks (as in the *Canopus in Argos* novels) Lessing stresses the ways in which group psychology, belief in political ideologies, and rhetorical language manipulate us. She values the dispassionate, curious, evaluative individual mind. Sufism provides a methodology for cultivating this type of mind, free of prejudice and propaganda.

Probably because of its emphasis on breaking through to new forms of consciousness, Lessing has described *The Golden Notebook* as her most Sufi book (Knapp 13). Literary critics also discuss elements of Sufism in the final two volumes of *Children of Violence*, in *Briefing for a Descent into Hell*, in *The Temptation of Jack Orkney and Other Stories*, and in *Memoirs of a Survivor* (Hardin; Seligman, "Sufi Quest"). Lessing continues to study Sufism in the eighties, evidenced by her many published reviews and introductions to the works of Shah and his colleagues.

Since the sixties Lessing has traveled extensively. She visited the United States in the late sixties and again in 1984. She has also visited the Soviet Union, Japan, Spain, Germany, and her childhood home, Southern Rhodesia, now Zimbabwe. Although Lessing maintains a healthy skepticism about liberation movements, she shows sympathy for the student radicalism of the sixties (Raskin). When she returned to the States in 1984, she visited several universities but refused to pander to Lessing scholars. She spoke of her support for the civil defense movement and for Robert Mugabe's government in Zimbabwe, her antipathy to communism, and her belief in God and in learning as the purpose for living (Berkowitz et al.). Some of Lessing's followers have been critical of her politics. Where is her radicalism? Where is her feminism? are the implicit questions of American audiences.

Lessing refuses to be a political leader of any ism, including feminism. For instance, she has often publicly censured the Soviet Union as one of the worst tyrannies of the modern world (Berkowitz et al. 8; Lessing, *Prisons* 22). She acknowledges that Socialist systems are as prone to elitism and tyranny as any other, if not balanced by critical, informed minds.

Nonetheless, Lessing continues her political interests. In 1982 she went on a lecture tour of Japan, in part to meet with the Atomic Cooperative about nuclear weapons (Broderick). Her writings also illustrate the importance of politics for her. In *A Ripple from the Storm* (1958) she examines the group process as it worked in an African Communist collective. *The Sentimental Agents* (1983) expresses her dismay with political rhetoric. *The Good Terrorist* (1985) is an ironic examination of terrorist activities and motivations in Britain. In *The Wind Blows Away Our Words* (1987) she looks closely at the plight of Afghanistan under Soviet repression.

Thus Lessing has never abandoned politics as her primary historical focus of study. She still believes in the need for "small informed groups who work for achievable goals independent of rhetoric" (Berkowitz et al. 8). But she does not shrink from naming tyranny, rhetoric, and force, no matter from what ideology they emerge. Awareness, an ironic distrust of institutions, and an informed historical perspective are typical of Lessing.

Doris Lessing now puts politics in the perspective of species survival. She has written a five-volume series, *Canopus in Argos*, which explores the future of planet Earth through an imaginary set of intrigues and struggles among fictional planets across a vast span of time. This global perspective on human survival began in *The Four-Gated City*, was echoed in *Memoirs of a Survivor*, and reaches its most fully developed form in the *Canopus* series. It is even implicit in the Jane Somers novels that focus on the survival of the elderly. Lessing believes that human evolution is the key. She states that as humans we have evolved and "we'll continue to do so if we don't blow ourselves up completely" (Bertelsen 118).

In 1984 Doris Lessing was sixty-five years old. She speaks of this period of her life as a time of freedom:

> I personally don't mind getting old. I think there's a great deal to be said for it. . . . when you become middle-aged . . . you literally be-come sort of unnoticed. You can just sit and watch and listen, and you don't have to put on any acts. . . . I sometimes think I belong to a sort of non-club . . . for people who like getting older, who like soli-tude. . . . We even have secret sorts of enjoyable meetings where we confess that we don't mind the thought of dying. . . . It gives you enormous freedom, you know, if you don't have to be terrified of all these things.   ("Interview," with Stamberg, 15)

Clearly this is a reflective period of her life. She went back to Zimbabwe in 1982, after a twenty-six-year absence, and visited her son John and her brother, Harry Tayler (Bertelsen 98–99). She paid close attention to black-white relations, to the political changes in the country, and to old landmarks. She wanted to visit her original home in Banket with her brother but did not go because of his anxiety about finding its remains.

In addition to revisiting her homeland, Lessing continues to reflect on her complex family. In 1984 and 1985 she published a two-part essay in *Granta* in which she attempts to come to terms with her mother and their relationship. She ends the first installment of this essay on a poignant note:

> Writing about my mother is difficult. I keep coming up against barriers, and they are not much different now from what they were then. She paralysed me as a child by the anger and pity I felt. Now only pity is left, but it still makes it hard to write about her. What an awful life she had, my poor mother! But it was certainly no worse than my

father's. . . . But I am not as sorry for him as I am for her. She never understood what was happening to her. ("Autobiography: Impertinent Daughters" 68)

Over the years of her career Lessing has attained an international stature. Her works are widely translated. She won the Prix Medici in 1976, the first British and first woman writer to do so. She won the Austrian State Prize for European literature in 1981 and the Hamburg Shakespeare Prize in 1982. She is frequently mentioned as a candidate for the Nobel Prize.

Lessing, though, rejects, even mocks, this recognition. She tried to expose the inner world of literary publishing by writing two pseudonymous novels under the name Jane Somers, *The Diary of a Good Neighbor* and *If the Old Could*. She wanted to "highlight that whole dreadful process in book publishing that 'nothing succeeds like success' " (Goodman; Yardley). In fact, the novels were refused by her two major British publishers. A third British publisher, Michael Joseph, who had also published her first novel, became suspicious and was taken into the ruse. Her American publisher, Alfred A. Knopf, was similarly suspicious and colluded with her.

Reviewers, however, did not recognize her writing. The books were not widely reported, and the reviews, Lessing says, were "brief" and "patronizing" (*Prisons* 52). Many of the writers were women journalists, obviously reviewing the book because they felt an affinity with Jane Somers, an alleged journalist-author. When the novels came out under Lessing's name in France and Scandinavia, however, the reviewers raved. When Lessing finally revealed her authorship, readers were congratulatory, while the publishers and reviewers were sour. Nonetheless, for an experienced writer to risk exposure to criticism by pseudonymous publishing takes conviction and courage. Although some accused her of a publicity stunt, others felt that such writing was really an exploration of questions of identity (Goodman; Yardley).

Doris Lessing resolutely refuses to become an institution. She is an independent thinker and a chronicler of human history. She is now dispassionate about personal reputation, power, and political ideologies, but she is deeply passionate about the development of the human species and the survival of the race. She reaches for new ways to use her experiences to make others see; she holds her own experience out, however, not as model but as method.

The Golden Notebook:
The African Background

Eve Bertelsen

Fictionalized as "Zambesia" in *Children of Violence* and as "the colony" in *The Golden Notebook*, Southern Rhodesia (now Zimbabwe) was Doris Lessing's home from 1925, when she was six years old, until she left for England at thirty, with her son, Peter, and the manuscript of her first novel, *The Grass Is Singing*. Like Anna Wulf's *Frontiers of War*, this work "treats the subject of racial injustice in modern Africa by focusing on the forbidden erotic relation between a white colonial and a black servant" (Draine, *Substance* 3).

Probably no one aspect of *The Golden Notebook* is more obscure to students than the geography and politics of Southern Rhodesia, which Lessing takes completely for granted. Since 1980, when newly elected Prime Minister Robert Mugabe declared Zimbabwe independent, the Rhodesia Lessing knew has become an increasingly hazy memory. Therefore some preliminary discussion of Rhodesian geography, history, and politics may be necessary. (For a map of contemporary Zimbabwe and Southern Africa, see *Maps on File*; for a map of Southern Rhodesia in 1962, see Legum 172; both are excellent for classroom use.)

The former Southern Rhodesia is a landlocked territory in the geographical area known as central Africa. The Zambezi River serves as its northern border with Zambia (formerly Northern Rhodesia), while the Limpopo in the south separates it from South Africa. It is bordered on the southwest by the state of Botswana and on the east and northeast by Mozambique.

A common mistake of Lessing's readers has been to conflate Southern Rhodesia with its neighbor South Africa. While from afar there may seem little to choose between the two regimes, they are in fact quite distinct. In South Africa white control has extended over three centuries of Dutch and British rule, with the Afrikaner government since the fifties consolidating the more informal racism of colonial times. For Rhodesia, by contrast, the colonial experience was fairly recent and short-lived. It was also entirely British. In spite of strong economic and strategic ties, Rhodesians always strenuously resisted proposals for incorporation into the Afrikaner republic "down south." Their relationship to Britain was also ambiguous. While the "home" culture of England was central to the identity of individuals and a taken-for-granted standard for "civilized" life, from the forties onward it became increasingly clear that Britain would be less likely than South Africa to support perpetual domination of the country's blacks, a strategy regarded by the settlers as essential to their very survival.

But the long memory of Rhodesia goes back centuries before colonialism. It begins with Great Zimbabwe, whose ruins and ancient gold mines white

colonists discovered early on as evidence of an African civilization long pre-
dating European conquest. Written records begin with the arrival in central
Africa in 1817 of Mzilikaze and his Ndebele (Matabele) tribe, refugees from
Zulu wars of conquest further south. In 1870 Mzilikaze was succeeded at
his capital, Bulawayo, by his son Lobengula, with whom the British entre-
preneur Cecil John Rhodes negotiated the mineral rights to Matabeleland
in 1888. Rhodes found a territory divided between the Shona, established
in the north and northeast, and the Ndebele, whose hegemony extended
from the midlands to the west and south. This tribal and territorial division
between Mashonaland and Matabeleland persists to the present day.

From this point events are determined by the classic two-pronged strategy
of colonialism wherever it occurs: the expropriation of the land and the
coercion of its inhabitants into wage employment as a cheap labor source.
In 1890 Rhodes returned, not with the ten white mining supervisors he had
promised, but with a Pioneer Column of 180 accompanied by 500 police,
intent on creating a British settlement in the area between the Limpopo
and the Zambezi rivers. The first task of the Pioneers was to put down angry
resistance by the Ndebele. They then in rapid succession occupied Bulawayo
in 1892, founded Fort Salisbury in Mashonaland, and, in 1895, renamed
Matabeleland and Mashonaland "Rhodesia."

Major rebellions by both tribes erupted in 1896. These were decisively
crushed and the chiefs submitted to white rule. Although the British government of the day was none too pleased with this new African adventure,
it empowered Rhodes and his commercial company, the British South Africa
Company, to run the country until 1923. A royal charter entitled the company
to raise taxes, pass laws, maintain a police force and administration, and
build roads and railways. During this time the foundations of Rhodesia were
firmly laid on the myths of the Pioneers: the peaceful white expedition had
found a land plagued by disease and intertribal strife; they had saved the
blacks from one another and put down a major revolt, thus establishing their
right of conquest; they had then endured the perils and hardships of carving
out a new life in an untamed land. Such were the enduring and self-evident
truths of white Rhodesia, which Doris Lessing would so mercilessly expose
in *The Grass Is Singing*, the early Martha Quest novels, and the African
stories.

In 1923 Britain annexed Rhodesia, immediately granting it "responsible
government" (the right to be a self-governing colony). Britain retained certain reserve powers, the most important being the right to veto legislation
discriminating against the African population. Not once in the subsequent
history of the territory were these powers invoked. White Rhodesians, left
to their own devices, proceeded to construct a legal apparatus that would
effectively keep the African in a subservient role. From 1890 to 1900, sixteen

million acres were handed out to white farmers regardless of whether or not Africans were occupying the land. Reserves were created in remote areas to absorb the displaced tribes. In these overcrowded and unproductive areas, the land deteriorated until even subsistence-level existence was problematic. In 1931 the Land Apportionment Act, which remained the centerpiece of the colony's segregation policies for the duration of white rule, formalized the division of land between white and black. It gave forty-nine million acres to fifty thousand whites and twenty-nine million acres to one million blacks, and it further stipulated that no African could own or occupy land in white areas.

Other laws were passed compelling Africans to serve white needs. A poll tax forced Africans into wage employment, thus ensuring a supply of cheap labor for white farms and mines. Pass laws controlled the movement of blacks in urban areas. The Masters and Servants Act made it a criminal offense for employees not to obey a "lawful" order of an employer. And the Industrial Conciliation Act prohibited Africans from qualifying for apprenticeships or skilled work and from joining trade unions. A Native Affairs Department administered every facet of African life, including agriculture, education, and medical and social facilities. Native commissioners had wide powers with regard to tax collection, the appointment of chiefs, the amalgamation or subdivision of tribes, and the trial of African civil and criminal cases. While the franchise remained technically nonracial, the qualifications based on income were so high that by 1948 only 158 blacks had the vote, compared with 47,000 whites. Education was left almost entirely in the hands of missionaries, whose moral influence was thought to be more effective and cheaper than hiring a police force. This last policy later recoiled on the administration, since mission stations, especially those run by the Anglican and Catholic churches, became sympathetic to the Africans' cause and later produced an entire generation of black nationalist politicians.

The African population on the whole, though, was effectively immobilized by this legislation and for half a century offered little organized resistance to the discriminatory system built up to contain them. The small elite that emerged from the earlier mission schools confined political activity to securing for themselves such privileges as were on offer, while farm laborers and unskilled industrial workers in the towns were debarred from any form of organization. It is in this context that we must understand the frustration of liberal and left-wing whites, like the "comrades" of the black notebook, in the face of the apparent passivity of the exploited and oppressed African population, represented in the novel by the Boothbys' cook, Jackson.

Administration during the colonial period may be simply summed up in three broad phases. From the 1930s until the mid-1950s the United Party of Godfrey Huggins, responsible for this legislation, ran the country on implicit "apartheid" lines. Then from 1954 to 1963 a brief period of "partnership" brought with it an economic boom, black economic advancement, and a limited degree of racial integration in public facilities. This policy was tied to the "Federation" of Southern Rhodesia with Northern Rhodesia and Nyasaland (which became, respectively, Zambia and Malawi in 1963), an arrangement that brought into Southern Rhodesia rich revenue from the copper mines of the north and worked almost entirely in the interest of Salisbury, the federal capital (now Harare). Rapid urbanization produced the first mass black organizations and a wave of demands that erupted in violent demonstrations. A white backlash against integration and violence swept Ian Smith's Rhodesian Front, an explicit apartheid party, into power in 1962 and the Federation was dissolved in 1963. In 1965 Smith, now prime minister, asserted Rhodesia's Unilateral Declaration of Independence from Great Britain (UDI). The country suffered a protracted racial and civil war that ended only when Britain intervened in 1979, forcing an open election. Robert Mugabe's Socialist ZANU party won a landslide victory, and Mugabe, as prime minister, declared Zimbabwe independent in April 1980.

Recent Zimbabwean scholars afford important insights into the character of Rhodesian society (Chennells; Steele, "Doris Lessing's Rhodesia"). They explore the contradiction between the heroic and egalitarian facade of the whites, who saw themselves as cultivated, adventurous, and classless, and the more modest reality: they were a motley group of middle-class British immigrants coexisting insecurely in a fairly rigid caste system with groups they regarded as "inferior"—Greek and Jewish traders and "poor white" Afrikaners from the south. Moreover, a series of economic slumps in the 1930s brought severe hardship to all but a few of the farming population, and even civil servants in the towns struggled to maintain the "civilized" life-style to which they felt entitled. While indisputably the whites' standard of living remained superior to that of the Africans, this more realistic description by contemporary scholars of the white community goes some way toward explaining the stridency with which racial difference was insisted on in the attempt to preserve status.

Economic adversity transformed the problem of acquiring African labor into something of an obsession, so that the terms *native problem* and *labor problem* may be read as synonymous. The reluctance of Africans to work for low wages on white farms led to various forms of compulsion and ill-treatment, such as physical punishment and the deprivation of wages for minor offenses. Whites persistently refused to acknowledge the capacity of blacks as peasant farmers in their own right, regarding their independent labor as yet another threat to white agricultural enterprises. Domestic servants likewise were bound by a rigid code of conduct, and fears of the "black peril" (attacks by black men on white women) were widespread, although incidents were virtually nonexistent. Because of the large number of single male farmers in the colony, miscegenation (cohabitation between white men and black or "colored" women) was more common, though severely frowned on as a threat to white identity. These relationships were equally unacceptable to blacks, who interpreted them as yet another instance of the exercise of arbitrary white power. Lessing's depiction in the black notebook of the Boothbys' relationship with their black cook and of George Hounslow's furtive liaison with his wife reflects this complex web of racial, sexual, and economic forces with uncanny accuracy.

In the more densely populated urban areas, segregationist practices were more obtrusive. Blacks lived under sufferance in squalid townships, supplying necessary services to a small elite of successful colonists who, in their clubs, hotels, and comfortable homes, pursued a way of life modeled on the "home culture." Relations between black and white repeated the fears and tensions of the rural scene. Steele offers an apt summary:

> Prewar Rhodesia was a conservative, highly rigid society, intolerant of criticism, especially from the outside. It was outwardly self-confident. It was also highly conformist and expected newcomers to conform. . . . Like other frontier societies it was also anti-intellectual. . . . At best it was paternalistic, at worst sadistic or neurotically suspicious towards Africans, but in all cases it denied them the rights to which they were entitled as human beings. ("Doris Lessing's Rhodesia" 48)

Labor and leftist politics in Rhodesia, especially during the war years depicted in *The Golden Notebook*, presents a picture of bitter rivalries and ideological conflicts that may best be understood as an impasse created by attempts to apply models of labor relations derived from advanced and industrialized European societies, especially Britain, to the situation of this underdeveloped and racially divided colony (Steele, "White Working Class Disunity").

A small Rhodesian Labour party modeled on the British Labour party and dominated by white industrial workers' unions had been established in 1928 and had for some time supplied opposition members in the legislative assembly. Though its constitution was not overtly racist, in effect it excluded black members, and it was designed to protect white artisans from the threat posed by cheaper black labor. Outmaneuvered by the government's own labor policies, the Labour party was all but defunct by 1936. In the late thirties, middle-class Socialists attempted to revive it along Fabian lines rather than as an agency for white trade unionism. When a major British Empire Training School for the Royal Air Force was opened in Salisbury early in 1940, left-inclined RAF men swelled the ranks of this group, the colony's sole focus of intellectual life.

The lines of battle on the left during the war years (as depicted sketchily in *The Golden Notebook* and more fully in *Children of Violence*, especially volume 3, *A Ripple from the Storm*) were drawn between members of the Rhodesia Labour party (RLP) who, following the policies of the home party in Britain, wished to retain the support of the unions, and the more radical wing (constituted as the Southern Rhodesia Labour party, or SRLP), which sought African participation. The Salisbury group of SRLP recruited into its executive the colony's small core of Fabian and Marxist intellectuals, including Lessing and her first husband. In her novels, Lessing is chiefly concerned with the inner workings of the SRLP and its public clashes in Congress with the RLP.

Rhodesian radicals faced a two-fold difficulty, philosophical and practical. First, orthodox Marxist analysis casts intellectuals in a vanguard role vis-à-vis an industrial proletariat, fueling the workers with ideas and organization that will enable them to exert a political presence and press their economic demands. But classical Marxist theory was inappropriate in a racially divided society where blacks were excluded not only from the unions but from all skilled labor. Serious class analysis in southern Africa had to wait until alternative models, drawn from comparable struggles in Cuba and China, became available to plot a course for the revolutionary transformation of colonial and peasant economies.

Second, and more immediately, if the Labour party was to exert any official pressure, it had to compete with Huggins's United party for the white vote. The split within the Labour party between the "left" SRLP, which held out against the odds for African membership, and the "right" RLP, which reverted to the party's original exclusivist position in order to capture the vote of white trade unionists, was unbreachable. Disunity in the party lost them the confidence of the electorate, and in 1946 both groups were trounced at the polls, leading to the demise of Labour as an opposition force.

But the Salisbury Left did not limit their activities to Labour party politics. They promoted Socialist ideas within a range of social welfare and intellectual organizations. In 1938 they founded a branch of the Left Book Club and a group called the Current Affairs Society. During the war they signed up some 250 members for the Rhodesian Friends of the Soviet Union and gained places on its steering committee. They also formed the Left Club, a more specialized group of hard-core Socialists, organized along disciplined "party" lines. There seems to be no evidence for the existence at this time of any Rhodesian Communist party as such, although certain individuals had links with the South African Communist party (SACP). While some of these groups were condoned by whites as part of the war effort (for example, a Medical Aid for Russia campaign), the radicals' strategy of infiltrating and achieving positions of leadership in a range of "front" organizations elicited strong disapproval. Rhodesia's modest core of leftists had their work cut out for them in their attempts simultaneously to save the Labour party for socialism and to generate a progressive culture in a moribund colonial town.

Lessing's black notebook creates a remarkable microcosm of wartime Rhodesia. The Boothbys' astonishingly English Mashopi Hotel is set in a humming tropical locale (probably Sinoia) complete with gum trees, locusts, cooing birds, and sizzling heat. Past its front veranda runs Rhodes's railway, and black peasants trudge the road to the mission and local reserve. Jackson, the model servant, works double shift, satisfying the needs of local farmers and their wives and playing "oppressed proletarian" to the weekending leftists. The Left group is itself representative: the indigent artisan George, the party hardliner Willi, the RAF men with their metropolitan critique, and Anna herself, sane and ironic, focalizing the action. Their youthful debates run through the whole spectrum of contemporary issues: frustration with colonial proprieties, the sheer exhaustion engendered by the endless "front" activities of their weekday lives, the faction fighting in the Labour party; the party's paralyzingly inappropriate theory; the nonexistence of that black proletariat they feel it is their destiny to lead.

And what, in the end, is achieved? Anna tells a sad tale of dissolution. Mrs. Boothby and Mrs. Lattimer are left in a state of neurotic collapse. Jackson is sent packing. George loses his dark lover and Anna her stern and restrictive mate. The cause seems lost, to them at least. Only the copulating insects remain to stare at the sun, and the pigeons who have escaped consumption continue to cleave the sky with silken wings. And in the heat the silent blacks toil on, more patient, perhaps, and more hopeful than the dialecticians that Africa will, one day, be free.

Politics and *The Golden Notebook*

Frederick C. Stern

If Rhodesia is terra incognita to college students in the nineties, leftist politics of the fifties are utterly mystifying. Differences between communism and Stalinism, factional infighting, the profound idealism of the left wing and its equally profound disillusionment over Stalin are facets of *The Golden Notebook* that often bring classes to a standstill in their reading. Thorough discussion of the political climate out of which the book was written facilitates reading and comprehension. Indeed, one way to describe *The Golden Notebook* is as a political novel, itself a complicated term. A good deal of contemporary theory, especially as influenced by Marxist thought, would insist that in some sense all works of art are political. At the very least, all art has or reflects a politics. But *The Golden Notebook* is political in another, more specific sense. Some of its manifest content is the role of politics in the lives of the "free women" it describes and in the lives of the characters imagined by Anna Wulf as writer. Thus, *The Golden Notebook* is a political novel not only because it has, reflects, or voices a politics but because it is *about* politics, especially post–World War II Left and Communist politics.

In countries of the West, many Communist parties had reached their greatest power shortly after World War I following what seemed hopeful signs for the worldwide Socialist movement that many saw in the Soviet Revolution of 1917. However, such success was short-lived. The ferocious struggles for power between Trotsky and Stalin and the subsequent political trials that took the lives of some of the best-known Soviet leaders, among them Kamenev and Zinoviev, as well as the defeat of revolutionary forces in such countries as Germany and Hungary, blasted the idealism of many leftists and caused havoc in the ranks of many Communist parties.

After Lenin's death, Leon Trotsky was Joseph Stalin's only serious rival in the contest for power in the Soviet Union, a struggle that Stalin won. Forced to flee the Soviet Union in 1929, Trotsky lived in various other countries before settling in Mexico, where he was assassinated in 1940. It is widely believed—though there has never been absolute proof—that his murderer was an agent of Stalin or his forces. The differences between Stalin and Trotsky were profound, ranging from the two men's personalities and backgrounds to such substantive matters as whether it was possible to have a Socialist revolution in one country alone, how the new state founded after the Soviet Revolution should be organized, and what role it should play. The split in Soviet communism between the two men led to a worldwide split. In most Western countries and, after World War II, in much of the Third World as well, there were two Communist parties. The larger of the two owed its allegiance to the existing Soviet state and hence to Stalin. The smaller, so-called Trotskyist parties opposed Stalin and Stalin's methods, considered the Soviet Union a "degenerate" form of Socialist society, and continued to espouse Trotsky's ideas—and sometimes split further over how to interpret these ideas. In England, during the period under discussion in *The Golden Notebook*, Trotskyism had found only a few followers and was viciously attacked as "Fascist" by Stalin-supporting Communists.

The Communist party of Great Britain (CPGB), founded in 1920, had far less base in the labor movement than did many other European parties. It accepted, in fairly short order, under the leadership of R. Palme Dutt and Harry Pollitt, the moves of the Communist International (Comintern) toward increasing "democratic centralism" (i.e., acceptance of the party's decisions without deviation—ostensibly after full discussion and vote) and other forms of discipline. "Prosperity," such as it was in the 1920s in some Western countries, including Britain and the United States, lessened interest in socialism. As a result, the Comintern encouraged such Western parties to engage in "legal" struggles, even in parliamentary and trade union work, rather than to foment revolution.

When the economic catastrophe that began in 1929 struck, the British and American parties had their largest periods of growth. By taking the lead in working-class movements for some forms of relief from the terrible hardships of the "crisis of capitalism," the two Communist parties became significant entities, though never large ones, in the body politic. One commentator writes that membership in the CPGB grew from a low point of 2,555 in late 1930 to 9,000 by 1932 (Dewar 220). The victories of some Fascist regimes (Germany, Hungary, Italy, and Spain) resulted in death, imprisonment, or involvement in underground struggles for thousands of Communist party members. Often Communists were the most courageous and determined fighters against fascism. Nowhere was this more dramatically evident than in Spain, where Francisco Franco, the Fascist general, militarily attacked a legally elected government in which Communists played a major role. In response, Communists and Socialists worldwide joined the International Brigade and came to Spain to fight on the side of the Spanish Loyalists. Such Spanish Communist leaders as La Pasionaria (Dolores Ibarruri) became heroes of the international left and democratic forces. It was only later that the internecine warfare on the Loyalist side among various forces—Communist, Trotskyist, and others—became widely known. Books like George Orwell's *Homage to Catalonia* (1939) were painfully disenchanting.

In World War II Communists and Socialists who opposed the German-led Fascist Axis joined together to fight the war, just as the Soviet Union, Britain, the United States, and other nations joined together (though Communists did not support the war until after the Hitler-Stalin pact was broken by Hitler's attack on the USSR). It is this moment, when the British and the Soviets were allies, that Lessing records in her African scenes. Communists had reason to hope for a worldwide turn to socialism after the Fascist defeat. Sometimes Western and other Communist parties were deeply involved with refugees from German nazism, like Willi, Anna's unpleasant lover in Africa.

With the end of the war, however, the Soviet-Western alliance dissolved. The United States had "the bomb," the Marshall Plan (an ostensible economic recovery program for Europe), and the Truman Doctrine (which, among other things, helped install a repressive regime of "colonels" in Greece), all of which seemed a threat not only to the Soviets but to Communists everywhere. In the United States, and to a much lesser extent in Britain, attacks on Communists increased. In the United States, the House Committee on Un-American Activities attacked not only Communists but many other leftists with complete disregard of constitutional protections (Black). Writers and other intellectuals were the committee's special targets, as Anna indicates in the blue notebook when she mentions "black-listed" screen writers (486). A group of Communist party leaders in the United States were convicted of "conspiracy to advocate the overthrow of the government" as Senator Joseph McCarthy's infamous witch-hunt escalated. Meanwhile, in Eastern Europe, Russia had occupied most of the countries that its armies had liberated from Fascist rule, and it had installed Communist party–dominated regimes. In 1948, Czechoslovakia, with its government of Communists and non-Communists headed by the Socialist Beneš, was taken over by Communist party forces in a coup.

Thus, in the 1950s, Communist party members in non–Eastern bloc countries, like Britain, saw the world as divided between the imperialists and antidemocrats, headed by the United States, and the forces of socialism, headed by the Soviet Union. The colonial world was in revolt against its Western overlords, economic problems were rife, the United States seemed bellicose. For Anna and Molly and many others, it was possible to be Communists and believe idealistically that they were fighting for justice, world peace, independence for colonial peoples—for a society more human and more humane than the present one.

Nonetheless, for some Western Communist intellectuals the adulation of Stalin was a problem—usually ignored for the sake of "the fight for peace and socialism." Anna has difficulties with Stalin's *Marxism and Linguistics* (Mills 301), which is discussed in her party writers' group (300). There were many other problems for Western Communists in the late forties and early fifties. For instance, Tito (Josip Broz), the leader of Yugoslavia, became the new major subject for Soviet attacks, as harshly excoriated as Trotsky had been in earlier years.

Furthermore, the power struggle in the USSR after Stalin's death (1953) eventually brought to power, not Beria, Malenkov, or Zhdanov, but Khrushchev, who was virtually unknown to Western Communists. This was a further source of unease. Revolutionary uprisings by workers against their Communist party–dominated states took place in the German Democratic Republic (East Germany) and most especially in Hungary. Soviet troops reentered the latter country on 4 November 1956, overthrowing the regime of Imre Nagy (who was soon executed) and installing, under Janos Kadar, a government the Soviets could accept.

But the worst blow of all, without question, was Nikita Khrushchev's speech on 25 February 1956, before the Twentieth Congress of the Communist party of the Soviet Union (Mills 365; Russian Institute 1). The speech, delivered to a closed session of the Congress, from which all foreign Communist party delegates were excluded, laid out many of the crimes committed by the Soviet state during Stalin's later years. Though Khrushchev dealt only with some of the worst offenses and though an effort was made to keep the speech secret for some time, it soon leaked. Party after party in the West had to come to terms by mid-1956 with what had to be acknowledged as fact—that many of the charges against Soviet society made in the West had been true.

The debate in England began officially with a statement by the Political Committee of the CPGB on 22 June 1956 (Russian Institute 173). Some CPGB leaders saw it as their task to contain the damage, and though membership dropped sharply, especially among writers, scientists, and other intellectuals, there was still strong defense of the Soviet Union by party leaders. Reflecting this development, Anna comments concerning a meeting at which "Comrade Harry" reports on the "terrible information" he has uncovered about what happened to Soviet Jews before Stalin's death (480). The reference is clearly to Hyman Levy, who had published his findings after being unable to get CPGB officialdom to do so, only to be roundly attacked by R. Palme Dutt (Levy). Doris Lessing, it should be made clear, was herself a contributor to the short-lived independent Marxist journal the *Reasoner*, founded by John Saville and the historian E. P. Thompson when it seemed impossible to break through official CPGB control of party discussion on this issue. She was also among "the intellectuals who are publicly known to have resigned from the Party, either at the time of the Hungarian uprising or shortly after the first of the year," a group that included Thompson, Saville, and, eventually, the historian Christopher Hill (Wood 202).

The particular political subject matter of *The Golden Notebook* is the breakup of the Left, especially the Communist Left, in the period following World War II, in particular after the revelation of Stalin's crimes. The remembered African sections of the novel, set during World War II, when Anna describes as the "real" basis for her novel *Frontiers of War* the incidents at the Mashopi Hotel, foreshadow the eventual breakup of the Communist

Left. The frame novel, "Free Women," charts the movement from the complete involvement of Anna Wulf in Communist party politics to her eventual estrangement from such activities. From the beginning of "Free Women," in the argument between Molly's ex-husband, Richard, on the one side and Anna and Molly on the other, we are apprised of the two women's previous Communist party politics. Even Richard, a financier, we discover, was a member of the Communist party for a brief period in the 1930s (16). Thus, from the "summer of 1957" opening of the first "Free Women" section, we are involved in discussion of left politics.

"Free Women" ends with rather wry admissions by Anna and Molly that they are now quite separated from such politics. Anna tells Molly that she is going to take a job as a marriage counselor and that she "is going to join the Labour Party and teach a night class twice a week for delinquent kids." Molly, who is about to get married to a "progressive" businessman, replies: "So we're both going to be integrated with British life at its roots" (665–66). The statement reflects the novel's concern about both the sexual and the professional lives of the women. It also reflects an end to their involvement with Communist and other far-left politics, an acceptance of the more "normal" parameters of British politics, and a diminution of the importance the women place on politics. Many intellectuals joined the Labour party, which at its foundation promised to embody Socialist values and goals within the British parliamentary system. At a time when the whole Western world appeared to be moving to the right, it was the logical choice for leftists wishing to stay involved in politics on some level. The Tory, or Conservative, party, similar in some ways to the American Republican party, was obviously not an option. The Liberal party, like the American Democratic party, would seem too firmly a part of the establishment and too reformist for Anna to consider.

One can argue, then, that one major theme of *The Golden Notebook*, embodied in "Free Women," is withdrawal from the Communist movement and the breakdown of that movement in the later fifties. The only other novel of merit I know that deals as extensively with this issue is the American novelist Clancy Sigal's *Going Away* (a work that can be read as a gloss on *The Golden Notebook*).

Throughout the novel, Communist politics dominates the lives of the major characters. Most of the men in Anna's life are Communists or ex-Communists, usually not English men, but Americans and continental Europeans, and they connect several issues in the novel. The Europeans—especially Michael—are deeply affected by the Stalinist executions that took place in East European countries during the earlier fifties. As Anna remarks in the red notebook, "Three of Michael's friends hanged yesterday in Prague" (159). This is the "Prague affair" Anna discusses with a party leader (161). The reference is to the execution in 1952—the same year in which many Jewish writers were executed in the USSR—of Rudolf Slansky, secretary of the Czech Communist party and a veteran Jewish revolutionary, and others for alleged spying for the United States and Israel. Some fifteen years later the frame-up was acknowledged by Czech and other Communist party leadership (Ettinger 1070).

In brief, Doris Lessing has written a novel in which the major characters are politically concerned, involved human beings. Most of them are growing profoundly disillusioned with communism, while remaining sharply at odds with Western "bourgeois" politics. They are thus often in conflict with both the Left and the "liberal"-to-right majority. It has been my intent in this essay to explore some aspects of history—especially Communist history— that are therefore crucial to an understanding not only of the "facts" but of the "feeling-tone" of *The Golden Notebook*.

Philosophical Contexts for *The Golden Notebook*

Jean Pickering

The difficulty of Lessing's fictions does not lie solely in Rhodesian history and colonial culture or in the leftist politics of the fifties. To the students in junior survey courses on twentieth-century British literature and in senior seminars on contemporary British women writers at California State University, Fresno, the philosophical concerns of the earlier twentieth century seem arcane, antiquated, or, at best, reducible to clichés. Since *The Golden Notebook* demands such a leap of the cultural imagination, my students, as must be true of comparable students everywhere, need an introductory discussion of the appropriate philosophical contexts, the most important of which are socialist realism, psychoanalysis, existentialism, and antipsychiatry.

Of these, the context that gives my students the most difficulty is socialist realism. Since they think of communism as an economic system whose primary aim is to undermine the Western way of life, they do not understand that it is mainly a theory of history in which aesthetics plays an essential part. Anna Wulf's observation that all Communists are novel writers (354) strikes them as out of character for revolutionaries, so they need first of all a summary of the place of art in Marxist thought. Because Marxist theory in its own view tends to the progressive, the scientific, the utilitarian, Marxists have tried to establish aesthetic theories stressing the usefulness of art, which may educate the populace about social injustice, offer "noble ideals for emulation," or help to organize collective labor (Thomson 8). Neither Marxism's conception of itself nor its social program explains why realism is the preferred literary technique.

Marx and Lenin both had an emotional attachment to the great nineteenth-century classics that prejudiced them in favor of realism. Although they recognized that the classics had been written by the bourgeoisie and, as "all art is class art," were therefore contaminated by bourgeois values, nonetheless they maintained that "all genuine art contains an objective reflection of at least some basic aspects of the life of the times. . . . This is the criterion of its realism and its social significance" (James 11, 10). The social significance of a work of art thus depended directly on its realism. The function of art was to further the cause of the working classes, eventually promoting a new proletarian culture. Lenin believed that "this new proletarian culture could not appear from nowhere . . . ; it must grow organically from what had gone before" (James 49).

Lenin's evaluation of the cultural heritage did not go unchallenged. In 1923 the LEF, the Left Front of the Arts, attacked realism because it fostered "the illusion that it was identical with reality" (Thomson 68). The founder of the LEF, the futurist poet Mayakovsky, believed that the culture of the past, as well as the society that produced it, should be destroyed. Trotsky's

Literature and Revolution (1923) is the best-known rebuttal of Mayakov-sky's position. MAPP, a conference of proletarian writers, objected to Lenin's emphasis on the classics, though they agreed that the working class "lacked even an elementary standard of culture" and that proletarian art "could not develop without the Party's guidance" (James 57–58). Both LEF and MAPP urged a greater emphasis on the future. In 1934, however, the First Congress of Soviet Writers formulated the socialist-realist tendency, which had been generally accepted during the twenties, as the officially sponsored method. This formulation of socialist realism, which is essentially Lenin's, persisted in Khrushchev's speech at the Third Writers' Congress in 1959, which reit-erated that the role of the artist "is to provide a positive model drawn from real life" (James 92).

Anna, for whom "Thomas Mann was the last of the writers in the old sense," notes that the contemporary novel has degenerated into reportage; the very realism that, in the Marxist view, justifies art has become for her the reason for the novel's current inadequacy: it "cannot create a new way of looking at life" (60, 61). Thus Anna's disillusionment with the Communist party has an artistic as well as a political basis.

Freudian psychoanalytic concepts in a popularized form are so familiar that students take them for granted. They know about the classical division of the psyche into the id, ego, and superego; about repression and the unconscious; about the importance of dreams. They have all heard of penis envy. They consider some of Anna's ideas about the psychological and sexual passivity of women (Deutsch 185–238) peculiar to the fifties, the kind of notions their mothers would have entertained. Although they are aware that Jungian analytical psychology is another form of the "talking cure," in general they are less familiar with its precepts. Most of them have heard of arche-types; some have in high school drawn mandalas as a prewriting exercise designed to put them in touch with the unconscious, but they are unsure about the ways in which Jung differs from Freud. A discussion of the two different approaches to dreams is a good place to start.

According to Freud, dreams are an important avenue *to* the unconscious; according to Jung, they are an important avenue *from* the unconscious. For Freud, the dream always needs interpretation, while for Jung the uncon-scious "appears in dreams in the naivest and most genuine way" (*Practice* 32). In addition to being the imaginary fulfillments of the "strong but re-pressed wish-impulse" (Freud 238), dreams may contain "ineluctable truths, philosophical pronouncements, illusions, wild fantasies, memories, plans, anticipations, irrational experiences, even telepathic visions" (Jung, *Practice* 147). When "disorientation occurs because life has become one-sided," dreams may point, for instance, "to present facts, marriage, or social position" that "the conscious mind has never accepted as sources of problems or conflicts" (43). Thus dreams give Anna insights she has overlooked in her daytime life, bringing such unwelcome news as that Michael will leave her.

Students' understanding of psychotherapy is typically based on the authoritarian rather than the dialectical model. They think of the "cure" of an illness rather the "task" of individuation, "in which the patient becomes what [he or she] really is" (Jung, *Practice* 10). Freudian psychology with its emphasis on the individual, on determinism and causality, on fixing whatever has broken down seems to fit more easily into their worldview than do Jungian principles, whose "aim is to bring about a psychic state in which [the] patient begins to experiment with his own nature—a state of fluidity, change, and growth where nothing is eternally fixed and hopelessly petrified" (46). Thus Jungian theory needs to be continually stressed in classroom discussions of *The Golden Notebook*.

Freud's view of the unconscious as a repository of repressed material is essentially negative and regressive. Jung, however, sees it as possessing both a "dark side" and a "good and positive" one; a collective unconscious, it has an innate connection with other human beings, containing "inherited instincts, functions, and forms peculiar to the ancestral psyche," which are "not inherited ideas, but possibilities of such ideas" (30, 34). These ideas may appear as archetypes, motifs, fairy tales (124), much as the Rumpelstiltskin figure, joy in destruction, occurs in different guises in Anna's dreams.

Jung's concern with continued growth in adulthood as opposed to Freud's emphasis on the lasting effect of infantile experience is particularly relevant to *The Golden Notebook*:

> A person in the second half of life . . . , to understand the meaning of his own individual life, needs to experience his own inner being. . . . Fully aware as he is of the social unimportance of his creative activity, he feels it more as a way of working at himself to his own benefit. Increasingly, too, this activity frees him from morbid dependence.
>
> (Jung, *Practice* 50)

This seems to describe both Anna's frame of mind and her final liberation from her writing block.

Most of my students have little acquaintance with existentialism. When introduced, it is very attractive to them—so much so that they become distracted by its many different versions. I therefore limit the discussion of existential ideas to Albert Camus's myth of Sisyphus and Simone de Beauvoir's feminism.

The central concept of Camus's thought is that of the absurd. Absurdity comes from the understanding that we are living a life without meaning:

"The absence of any profound reason for living . . . separates humanity from the universe; this divorce between man and his life is properly the feeling of absurdity" (*Myth* 6). Try as Anna will to maintain her contact with the universe, she is constantly afflicted by this very feeling: her political disillusions, her writer's block, the departure of the man she loves have rendered her life absurd. She believes, in Camus's words, that "the purest of joys . . . is feeling" (103), but her capacity to feel has been stultified because both her political heroes and her lover have abandoned her. What Camus calls "the absurd joy par excellence," creation, is denied by her writer's block, the consequence of her multiple deprivations in both public and private life.

Like Camus, Anna seems to believe that "everything begins with consciousness and nothing is worth anything except through it" (Camus 13). Far from trying to escape through oblivion, she attempts to make herself more conscious: using a form that is itself recommended by Camus (70), she documents her fragmentation in her notebooks while at the same time recording her attempt to sharpen her consciousness. Thus she engages in the existential "unceasing struggle" to confront the absurd (Camus 31).

Camus sees Sisyphus as the epitome of the absurd hero who "knows the whole extent of his wretched condition. . . . The lucidity that was to constitute his torture at the same time crowns his victory" (121). The sense of the absurd is founded on "this mind and this world straining against each other without being able to embrace each other" (40), a statement that nicely describes Anna's condition. Lessing, however, is not absolutely without hope. In the interior "Golden Notebook," Anna adds a progressive touch to the myth of Sisyphus, telling Saul Green, "There's a great black mountain. It's human stupidity. There are a group of people who push a boulder up the mountain. When they've got a few feet up, there's a war, or the wrong sort of revolution, and the boulder rolls down—not to the bottom, it always manages to end a few inches higher than when it started" (627–28).

Lessing's modification is not without some foundation in Camus's thought, for his worldview affords a special role for the artist, whose "very vocation, in the face of oppression, is to open the prisons and to give a voice to the sorrows and joys of all. . . . Any authentic creation is a gift to the future" (212).

As Camus's constant use of *man* to refer to the entire human race suggests, the special problems of woman's authentic existence escape his attention. Simone de Beauvoir's *Second Sex* deals with them in detail. Because woman has always been subordinate, "she is defined and differentiated with reference to man, and not he with reference to her; she is the incidental, the inessential as opposed to the essential. He is the Subject, he is the Absolute—she is the Other" (Beauvoir xvi). Pointing out that the condition of being the subject of one's own universe seems to be the natural state, Beauvoir seeks to answer the question of why women have accepted the condition of object and other.

As the second-class status of women seems to be innate, it lacks the contingent nature of a historical fact, which like slavery or the oppression of the proletariat might be subject to change (xviii). Since "the division of the . . . sexes is a biological fact, not an event in human history," women have no real way of "organizing themselves into a unit that can stand face to face with the correlative unit" (xix). Dispersed among their menfolk, women are attached more firmly to men than they are to other women (xix), as Anna and Molly have cause to note. To renounce the advantages that accrue to an alliance "with the superior caste," "to decline to be the Other," would be to surrender advantages without acquiring economic and psychological liberty in return (xx–xxi).

The idea of liberty is the key concept in Beauvoir's thought. In existentialist ethics,

> every subject achieves liberty only through a continual reaching out toward other liberties. There is no justification for present existence other than its expansion into an indefinitely open future. . . . Every individual concerned to justify his existence feels that his existence involves an undefined need to transcend himself, to engage in freely chosen projects. (xxviii)

This "indefinitely open future" is precisely what is denied to woman because, although "a free and autonomous being like all human creatures," she finds herself compelled to play the object to the man's subject. Thus "women on the whole *are* today inferior to men; that is, their situation affords them fewer possibilities. The question is: should that situation continue?" (xxiii–xiv).

Although this question underlies their discussions of the relations between the sexes, Anna and Molly seem to have accepted women's alterity for much the same reasons that Beauvoir gives for its having arisen in prehistoric times. Because maternity involves natural functions, it does not confer transcendence, and "the domestic labors that fell to [woman's] lot because they were reconcilable with [it] imprisoned her in repetition and immanence" (Beauvoir 57–58). Anna in particular has internalized her status as other, even believing in the vaginal orgasm, an idea without biological foundation promulgated by Freud because of his need to explain female sexuality in terms of male anatomy.

If existentialism attracts my students, antipsychiatry fascinates them, even though the recent increase in mentally ill street people makes R. D. Laing less persuasive to the current generation.

Existential thought, particularly that of Sartre, was a major influence in the development of R. D. Laing's antipsychiatry. His first book, *The Divided Self* (1960), is subtitled *An Existential Study in Sanity and Madness*. The main concept, "ontological insecurity," a version of existential anxiety, is in his view the prime cause of schizophrenia: the ontologically insecure individual "may feel more unreal than real . . . , precariously differentiated from the rest of the world, so that his identity and autonomy are always in question" (42). The schizophrenic "is not able to experience himself 'together with' others or 'at home in the world' . . . ; [nor does he] experience himself as a complete person but rather as 'split' in various ways"; typically the schizophrenic divides the self into an inner self and a false self, constituted by the playing of a part imposed from outside (17, 73). The false self, originally constructed to protect the inner self, ultimately cuts it off from feeling: "the whole inner world comes to be more and more impoverished, until the individual may come to feel he is merely a vacuum" (75). Laing maintains that this way of being has become commonplace, indeed typical, of the individual in contemporary society. The inability to feel that he describes is precisely the kind of alienation that causes Anna's writing block.

By 1967, when he published *The Politics of Experience*, Laing had adopted the stance Lessing anticipated in *The Golden Notebook*: schizophrenic behavior is "*a special strategy that a person invents in order to live in an unlivable situation*" (*Politics* 79). This "psychotic condition may enable one to overcome a deep rift in the human personality, characteristic of 'normal' people in our type of society" (Sedgwick 97). Typically this healing comes about through a "voyage into inner space and time," which is accompanied by a sense of "ego-loss, or death, [together with] feelings of the enhanced significance and relevance of everything" (*Politics* 103, 105). Laing goes on to suggest that "we can no longer assume that such a voyage is an illness that has to be treated . . . : *this voyage is not what we need to be cured of, but . . . is in itself a natural way of healing our own appalling state of alienation called normality*" (116). So too "the dynamic of *The Golden Notebook* pushes . . . Anna Wulf towards a state of saving schizophrenia—a state that permits her commitment to practical goals, visionary ideals, art, work, social organization, logic, and order, while at the same time allowing her to acknowledge and even honor all that accompanies chaos—creation, destruction, randomness, power, potential, vitality, and emotion" (Draine, *Substance* 88).

Ultimately the most difficult task for students lies not in grasping the essence of any of these philosophical contexts but in holding them all in their minds at the same time. They tend to favor one or another as temperament and experience move them. Thus they resist the idea that Lessing means to be all-inclusive—that these contexts are not systems applied after the fact as Ernest Jones applied the Oedipus complex to *Hamlet* but are integral to Lessing's conscious intention; in short, that the meaning of *The Golden Notebook* lies in the juxtaposition of conflicting ideas, that we must learn to see it whole, just as Anna taught herself to visualize simultaneously both the smallest creature in a drop of water and the entire world.

The Principal Archetypal Elements of *The Golden Notebook*

Lorelei Cederstrom

One of the main difficulties in teaching *The Golden Notebook* involves coming to terms with its fragmented structure and with the confusing contradictions in the protagonist's descriptions of the other characters. Instructors can deal with these problems by approaching the novel from a Jungian perspective.[1] From this critical base, the book can be read as the depiction of an archetypal rite of passage. The protagonist, Anna Wulf, is undergoing a process of psychological development that begins with the breakdown of her defenses against certain frightening realizations. The dangerous vulnerability of Anna's ego is evident in the fragmentation of her conscious personality, in her difficulties in maintaining a persona, or social facade, and, most significantly, in the irruption of archetypal elements of the unconscious into her ordinary life. Through entries in the blue notebook, her diary, we also learn that Anna is suffering from a writer's block brought on by her refusal to deal with the dark side, the shadow, of her impulses and the world in which she lives. The diary and the three other notebooks reveal that Anna's psychological problems are individual and collective; she is fighting both a personal and a political battle in a search for wholeness. Through a great effort of will and the division of herself into four rigid modes of perception, reflected in the four notebooks she keeps, Anna is attempting to shore herself up against the immanent flooding of her conscious personality by that which she most fears—chaos and an anarchic will to destruction.

As her fragile ego and its defenses break down, Anna begins the pattern of psychological transformation that Carl Jung calls the "process of individuation." Through this process, Anna is forced to confront all the personal and collective demons that she had, until now, held at bay. According to Jung, individuation is the development of a unified psyche through the creation of a link between one's conscious life—the world of the ego and the persona—and the darker shadows of the unconscious. The goal, in Jungian terms, is to develop an archetypal "self." By confronting and assimilating oppositions within the psyche, the self becomes a bridge between the conscious world with its social imperatives and the deepest needs of the unconscious. In *Ego and Archetype*, the Jungian Edward Edinger describes the self as "the ordering and unifying center of the total psyche (conscious and unconscious) just as the ego is the center of the conscious personality" (3). Anna Wulf eventually develops an integrated and functioning self. Before that occurs, however, she searches for wholeness through social relationships. Seeking a positive relationship with a man, she becomes involved in a series of self-destructive affairs with men who are even more divided than she is. Hoping to make a difference in the world, she works for the Communist party but finds political activities increasingly irrelevant. Anna's writer's block is a direct result of her frustration; once a published novelist, she has ceased to write at all rather than use the novel to reflect the fragmentation and despair she has found in both personal and political relationships in the modern world. By the end of the novel, however, Anna has managed to overcome her frustration and despair. This is evident in a newfound personal strength and the restoration of her creativity through the publication of a novelette, the "Free Women" sections of *The Golden Notebook*. Anna's process of individuation is complete when she develops a self that can withstand the forces of disintegration that threaten her from within and without.

A central element in the Jungian framework of the novel is the depiction of Anna's relationship with Mrs. Marks, a Jungian analyst, to whom she has turned in an attempt to find relief for the pain of everyday life and a means of unifying the divisions within herself that are blocking her creativity. The relationship with Mother Sugar, as Anna calls her, is difficult since Anna is reluctant to apply the analyst's advice. As a Jungian, Mrs. Marks continually refers Anna back to the archetypal patterns that shape human experience. She teaches her to "name" the archetype that emerges in persons or situations as a means by which they can be controlled. At first, Anna rejects the idea that her experiences are anything but unique (471); she deliberately fails to see the applicability of archetypal patterns to her situation and remains at the mercy of her deepest fears. Slowly, however, Anna accepts Mrs. Marks's suggestions. She learns to counter her most negative fears with a positive image. In so doing, she finds within herself an analytical consciousness built on the assimilation of contradictions in her nature. She discovers this strong Anna, the unifying self, in a dream: "I was myself . . . yet there was a personality apart from the Anna who lay asleep. . . . It was a person concerned to prevent the disintegration of Anna" (614). Later, she calls this the "disinterested person" and the "controlling personality." The new Anna appears at the end of her psychological journey, but before the completed self emerges, Anna must name and assimilate all the darkness within.

In the course of her movement toward an integrated selfhood, Anna is confronted by several archetypal figures. Each is a projection of the collective unconscious, a universal figure that occurs during the process of individuation. As such, each represents qualities Anna does not wish to acknowledge as part of herself, so she sees them, instead, embodied in dreams or personified in others. In her personal life, Anna struggles with archetypal configurations that Jung calls the shadow and the animus. In her political life, she must come to terms with the Jungian wise old man, or great father. During individuation, Anna has a recurring dream about another common archetypal figure, the threatening dwarf. A very complex figure in the novel, this archetype menaces Anna in both her personal and political life. Each of the Jungian archetypes that confront Anna is at once universal and unique, demanding careful attention in relation to Anna's individuation.

The shadow is one of the first personifications of the unconscious encountered during the process of individuation. It represents the hidden side of one's personality that is projected onto a person of the same sex. This figure appears throughout the novel, but it is presented with a slightly different emphasis each time it occurs. As Anna changes she is confronted with a different aspect of the shadow until all its dark faces are recognized as her own. A large part of Anna's yellow notebook consists of an unfinished novel, "The Shadow of the Third." In this fictional account of her alter ego, Ella, and of Ella's affair with a married man, Paul, Anna confronts several aspects of her hidden self. The "third" in the story is Paul's wife, on whom Ella is projecting her own positive shadow. Ella sees the wife as a "serene, calm, unjealous, unenvious, understanding woman . . . self-sufficient, yet always ready to give happiness when it is asked for." Ella knows that this is not a realistic portrait but, rather, "is what she would like to be herself; this imagined woman is her own shadow, everything she is not" (207). Instead of working on herself to create a strong Ella who can live without Paul, she is using her positive image of Paul's wife as an excuse for her own weakness. In her refusal to grow, Ella reflects Anna's unwillingness to face reality. As the dark side of "free" Anna, Ella reveals a masochistic weakness in all her relationships with men as well as an inability to confront the painful conflicts between her sexual needs and the demands of motherhood. Anna avoids coming to terms with the self-defeating tendencies in her relationships, particularly in her affair with Michael, by relegating these weaknesses to Ella. Nonetheless, by fictionalizing her dark side, Anna is beginning to use her shadow creatively. Through Ella, Anna comes to understand those qualities that have led her into dependent relationships and learns to express her sexual needs instead of continuing to allow her needs to be defined by the men around her.

Another stage in the realization of the shadow takes place in the penultimate section of the novel, "The Golden Notebook." Here, Anna recognizes the importance of the creative imagination as a means of objectifying and assimilating her dark side. Ella, as a "shadow in the willed imagination" (546), not only reflects weaknesses but can bring positive strengths into existence. Anna learns that the ultimate value of her fiction lies in the possibility that "these marvellous, generous things . . . in our imaginations could come in existence, simply because we need them, because we imagine them" (637). Anna leaves Ella unfinished, waiting to take on a more positive shape. Until that shape forms, Ella is an inadequate defense against the realities of personal and social disintegration that confront Anna daily. Her fictional creation must wait until Anna sees more clearly what she wants and needs.

Anna was attempting to deal with her shadow through her fictional Ella since the ordinary means of control were breaking down. In normal circumstances, the shadow is kept at bay through the offices of the persona, the social personality that enables one to function in the world. Without a job and without the ability to write for publication, Anna had attempted to create a strong persona through her work for the Communist party. In her red notebook, she notes that she had joined the party to put an end to "the split, divided, unsatisfactory way we all live" (161). The repressions and assassinations of the Stalin regime in the Soviet Union have shaken her belief in the Communist ideal. Anna makes one of her most difficult decisions, to leave the party, only when she becomes more interested in personal matters than political issues. Canvassing, Anna discovers lonely, frustrated women eager to talk to anyone who knocks at their doors. She cannot change anyone's political orientation but instead finds herself providing a social outlet for these dissatisfied women. Within the party, she discovers that virtually everyone she knows is also personally dissatisfied. This feeling is expressed through a covert creativity. Again and again, her comrades speak of controversial manuscripts that they have hidden away in drawers. The party, thus, adds self-censorship to their already "divided and unsatisfactory" lives. This realization supports Anna's own reluctance to write for publication since she can offer no unifying vision. Anna learns as well that the devoted party workers share an illusion: each dreams of a special recognition from Stalin, the "great father." Anna finds an unwillingness among party members to criticize Stalin or his policy statements because of their absorption in the archetypal image of the great father. No matter what the evidence, real knowledge is betrayed by blind faith in the dream. "How odd," Anna notes, "we all have that need for the great man and create him over and over again in the face of all other evidence" (163). It is when Anna "names" Stalin as the great father, the archetypal wise old man, that she understands why her comrades have been unable to criticize the criminal activities in Russia. Her final writings in the red notebook confirm this insight; she has recognized that her dream of the world party as a magnificent, unified red "fabric" was the creation of her imagination out of a need for wholeness (198–99). In her dream she feared tugging at the loose thread that would destroy the fabric, but in life she can no longer suppress her criticisms out of love for the great father. Anna describes the sense of loss and defeat she feels when leaving the party, for despite its failures, the party provided a collective support for her fragile sense of self.

Establishing a unified personality involves coming to terms with both the realm of the collective consciousness, the social-political world, and the realm of the collective unconscious, the hidden aspects of the self, if the ego is to avoid being submerged by one or the other. Although Anna has been absorbed in her political activities for many years, she has not yet confronted the full power of the realm of the collective unconscious. She has glimpsed that world in dreams but closed it off in fear, for great courage is needed to deal with the disintegration that precedes rebirth. The drive toward wholeness, however, is bringing her ever closer to that confrontation. Anna has already realized the inadequacy of her two main defenses: her alter ego, Ella, remains an unfinished fiction in the yellow notebook, and her red notebook is closed when she leaves the party. Anna's individuation demands that she now confront the most powerful archetypal figures of the unconscious she has denied for so long.

The most important Jungian archetype that Anna confronts is the animus. Like the shadow, the animus is born out of one's deepest, most hidden needs, but it is projected, always, on a member of the opposite sex. The powerful animus is potentially either a creator or destroyer. Each person carries within the self an image of the other, a being of the opposite sex who must be recognized as part of oneself in order to complete the personality. Jung writes that the psyche grows toward individuation by the assimilation of oppositions, including the sexual polarities that permeate our lives and culture. The "man within," in Anna's case, is projected on Saul Green, Anna's American boarder. Even before Saul moves into her flat, Anna is on the verge of total disintegration. She is unable to write, full of anxiety, incapable of forming a vital sexual relationship, and troubled about the world at large. At the same time, Anna recognizes none of these failures as her own; instead she projects them and sees them personified in Saul. Anna and Saul become involved in a life-and-death struggle as the old Anna is destroyed in order that a new Anna can be created. Their relationship is characterized by childish quarreling and the surfacing of personalities that neither would recognize as their own under ordinary circumstances. As she struggles with Saul, Anna lets go, one by one, of the old personalities that she had used in dealing with men. As role after role disappears, Anna searches for the core of herself that remains. The struggle and the search invade her dreams as well as her waking life. Since Saul reflects an inner image, it is not surprising that their struggle should also dominate her sleep. In her dreams, she and Saul eventually play "against each other every man-woman role imaginable" including roles Anna had rejected in life (604). In a desperate attempt to find an Anna that endures through all the roles, Anna remembers the advice of Mrs. Marks about countering fearful images in dreams with powerful positive forms. Struggling through the intense relationship with

Saul, Anna begins to assert a new self capable of dreaming of deliverance from disintegration (600). She accepts, at last, Mrs. Marks's diagnosis that Anna is suffering from a writer's block. This admission is such a psychological triumph that Anna can close her four notebooks and bring all the fragmented parts of herself together, symbolically, in her single golden notebook, which forms the concluding section of the novel. The final assimilation of the animus is recorded in this inner "Golden Notebook." Anna is prepared psychologically to send Saul away, but before he leaves, he becomes the means by which her creativity is restored. As the personification of the creative aspect of the animus, it is appropriate that Saul gives Anna the first sentence of her "Free Women" novelette.

Like the animus, the dwarf, which appears in a recurring dream, is a crucial archetypal figure in Anna's process of individuation. In her dreams this figure is threatening; she sees it as "pure spite, malice, joy in malice, joy in a destructive impulse." Anna notes that she has this dream when she can feel that the "walls" of herself are "thin or in danger." The figure goes through several alterations; it is a vase, an elf, an old man or woman, but it is always "lively," despite its deformity (477). Mother Sugar forces Anna to see that this creature can be positive as well as negative for, as a Jungian, she recognizes this archetype immediately. Jolande Jacobi in *Complex/Archetype/Symbol* notes that like Rumpelstiltskin, the dwarf is a "spirit goblin, a *Kabeiros*, an archetypal figure whose alluring 'help' brings ruin to woman, and threatens what is most precious to her but, precisely because she has recognized and named it, releases her from its power and leads to salvation" (101). Anna has a great deal of difficulty in naming this figure. In particular, she prefers to see it as an abstraction rather than embodied in a living being (479). Despite her desire to prevent its personification, she recognizes in another dream that its "smile of joyful spite" is on her own face. By understanding that the anarchic principle, the dwarf, is a part of her being, Anna touches on the deepest and most serious level of the shadow. Erich Neumann in *Depth Psychology and a New Ethic* notes that before confrontation with the shadow, the ego rests "serenely in a complacent identification with all that is good in human nature." This complacency is shattered when the shadow reveals the evil of its dark face as a mirror reflection of the known face. Neumann explains that a common pattern in the confrontation between the ego and the shadow is the occurrence of a number of dreams in which "this other confronts the ego in such guises as the beggar or cripple, the outcast or bad man. . . ." These dreams eventually lead to the recognition that "the other side in spite of its undoubted character of hostility and alienness to the ego, is a part of one's own personality." Through this confrontation, the "old idealized images" of oneself are replaced by a "perilous insight into the ambiguity and many-sidedness of one's own nature" (79).

Through the dwarf, Anna sees the many faces of the self. After the dream in which she names her shadow as herself, she asks, "So now I am the evil vase; next I'll be the old man-dwarf; then the hunch-backed old woman. Then what?" The answer she hears—"the witch, and then the young witch!"—reminds her of the means by which she can deal with her shadow (496). Anna recalls a dream in which she saw Mrs. Marks as an "amiable witch" (250), a powerful figure she can call to her aid whenever she is threatened. By seeing herself as the young witch, she is acknowledging the growth of her own power, an inner strength with which she can control evil. The ability to control chaos and avoid destruction is the culmination of Anna's individuation. In the golden notebook Anna amplifies her central realization. She acknowledges the special kind of courage that is "at the root of every life" but recognizes that it exists because "injustice and cruelty is at the root of life" as well (636). Similarly, through the dwarf, Anna learns that destruction and chaos are a part of her because creativity and order are also a part of her. Jung writes about the development of wholeness through the assimilation of such oppositions: "There is no light without shadow and no psychic wholeness without imperfection. To round itself out, life calls not for perfection but for completeness" (*Psychological Reflections* 315). As a completed self, Anna need not fear either the disorder of the world or her own anarchic impulses, for she has learned that both can be controlled by the equally powerful forces within.

This essay presents merely the most basic information regarding the Jungian patterns in Lessing's novel. The book is permeated, throughout, with Jungian symbols and archetypal figures. Even an examination as brief as this, however, reveals that Lessing is providing a paradigm for the patterns of development in the feminine psyche. She describes the painful process of disintegration that precedes the development of a unified self, and she reveals the complexities of the conscious and unconscious forces at work on the psyche of the creative woman in the twentieth century. In addition, *The Golden Notebook* provides a many-faceted examination of the relation between psychological processes and creative processes and between the power of the political imagination and the creative intuition. The process of individuation offers a context for the discussion of the interaction of all these elements in a work that remains an intricate and complex masterpiece of world literature.

NOTE

[1]Most of the Jungian structures that Lessing uses are straightforward and can be defined in the context of the novel. However, students or professors desiring an

introduction to Jungian psychology may consult either of two readily available paperbacks: Carl G. Jung, ed., *Man and His Symbols* (New York: Dell, 1973), or Calvin S. Hall and Vernon J. Nordby, *A Primer of Jungian Psychology* (New York: Signet-NAL, 1973).

The Golden Notebook as a Modernist Novel

Marjorie Lightfoot

Situated somewhere between modernism and postmodernism, *The Golden Notebook* can benefit from a modernist reading that draws parallels with texts and contexts familiar at least to upper-level English majors. Thus, teaching Doris Lessing's *Golden Notebook* (1962) by allying it to such famous works as T. S. Eliot's *Waste Land* (1922) and James Joyce's novel *Ulysses* (1922) offers a perspective often known to college students by the time they take a twentieth-century British literature or women's studies course. If, however, modernism is new to them, teaching them about it provides a helpful vantage point for understanding *The Golden Notebook*.

Virginia Woolf wryly observed that "in or about December, 1910, human character changed" ("Mr. Bennett" 320); this change is reflected in the experimental British literature of World War I, the twenties, the depression, World War II, and the "sadly diminished age" that ended modernism by 1965 (Holman). Self-exiled, Eliot left the United States; Joyce, Ireland; Lessing, Rhodesia. Like *The Waste Land* and *Ulysses*, *The Golden Notebook* reveals the fragmentation and alienation felt in the twentieth century—war torn, materialistic, superficial, sterile. Fredric Jameson calls the modernist crisis "that dissociation of the existent and the meaningful, that intense experience of contingency" offering a choice of two ideologies, nihilism or existentialism, with modernism for an aesthetic (129–30).

Eliot's symbolist poem, Joyce's epic and mythic work, and Lessing's philosophical novel search for meaning. But spiritually arid people in *The Waste Land*, unable to fuse thought and feeling, suffer a "dissociation of sensibility" (Eliot, "Metaphysical Poets" 517) that affects self-integration and communication with others. Likewise, in *Ulysses* the intellectual, Stephen Dedalus, and the sensuous everyman, Leopold Bloom, feel isolated and alienated. *The Golden Notebook* depicts the creative person's blocked sensibility as the self becomes divided by narcissism and disgust and dissociated from others (A. Carey 233–34). Fearing that malice rules modern life, people like Anna Wulf oscillate hopelessly between alienation from society and victimization within it. William A. Johnsen believes that "the real project of modern literature" is to replace this futile flux with a willingness "to learn from contemporaries and predecessors as well as teach them, how to imagine a non-sacrificial society" (20). People can escape useless shifts between self-isolation and participation as victim or victimizer in society only if they will help one another use the experience of the past and the present to imagine a more positive future—and then work to create it.

As Eliot realizes:

> Our civilization comprehends great variety and complexity, and this
> variety and complexity, playing upon a refined sensibility, must pro-

duce various and complex results. The poet must become more and more comprehensive, more allusive, more indirect, in order to force, to dislocate if necessary, language into his meaning. ("Metaphysical Poets" 517).

Elsewhere, Eliot suggests that artists should depersonalize their art to allow their minds to "digest and transmute the passions which are [the mind's] material" into works that will reflect and echo "the mind of Europe" ("Tradition" 509).

Eliot, Joyce, and Lessing are not identified as the narrators in their work. Techniques of indirection—authorial distance, structure, style, personae, archetypal images, motifs, allusion, juxtaposition, ellipsis, and irony—foster the modernist's detachment, while implying a commentary.

Joyce's persona in *A Portrait of the Artist as a Young Man*, Stephen Dedalus, says, "The artist, like the God of the creation, remains within or behind or beyond or above his handiwork, invisible, refined out of existence, indifferent, paring his fingernails" (215). In *Ulysses* an impersonal voice or voices constantly change styles. Ironically, this narrative multiplicity "actually draws attention to the author who is so shy of being his own narrator" (Sultan 144). That is true of all modernist works in which form is self-consciously contrived. Joyce's protean styles, like Eliot's and Lessing's, suggest that truth is hard to grasp, that conventional language and structure are inadequate to communicate. In *The Golden Notebook* we are not told who has enough faith that words communicate meaningfully to organize sections of the protagonist's notebooks and "Free Women" novel for publication (Lightfoot 282). But an impersonal editor notes such information as dates and the publication of Saul's novel, and the protagonist controls many shifts of style.

What David Hayman says of *Ulysses* is apt for the other two works:

> Many separate voices contribute to a unified and coherent second creation, and we can trace paths through the labyrinth without losing the dramatic narrative they must serve. . . . as in a symbolist poem, the objective universe of *Ulysses* is frequently glimpsed *through the medium* (i.e., the style itself) and *in terms* of it rather than *in* the novel, and our pleasure is drawn from the process of apprehending what happens, the meaning of what happens, and the expression which is in itself an event. (20, 22)

Students enjoy not only putting together such a complex jigsaw puzzle but recognizing the pieces available, relating them to one another, and supplying missing pieces, to reveal pictures within the total picture. A modernist puzzle about life involves a search for hidden treasure, and neither the pursuit nor the goal is trivial. Eliot, Joyce, and Lessing each contrive a formal world to contain the quest.

For *The Waste Land*, the title, plan, and much of the symbolism of the grail quest came from Jessie L. Weston's *From Ritual to Romance*; James G. Frazer's *Golden Bough* allied the Fisher King of Arthurian romance to ancient tales of vegetation gods (*Waste Land* 457). Comparison of Jungian archetypal characters reveals that spiritual sterility threatens modern humankind. Using many styles, the poem parodies, quotes, and misquotes literature, history, and myth. Resulting juxtapositions evoke such ironies as the "Goonight" of insensitive modern drunks leaving a pub, opposed to the gracious farewell of grief-stricken, suicidal Ophelia.

In "*Ulysses*, Order and Myth" Eliot, recognizing kinship, acknowledged Joyce's method of "manipulating a continuous parallel between contemporaneity and antiquity" as a means of "controlling, of ordering, of giving a shape and a significance to the immense panorama of futility and anarchy which is contemporary history. . . . [Joyce's method] is, I seriously believe, a step toward making the modern world possible in art." The very title of *Ulysses* forces us to perceive the work in the epic tradition and consider Homer's hero and Joyce's protagonist in each other's light. Joyce actually follows the structure of *The Odyssey* only very roughly (Sultan 21). David Hayman considers *The Odyssey* and *The Divine Comedy, Hamlet*, and *Faust*, along with mock epics like the *Satyricon, Gargantua and Pantagruel*, and *Tristram Shandy*, to be Joyce's principal models (19–21). Philip Brockbank finds Joyce's "parodies prove his capacity to live in the past even as he disengages from it," which is what Eliot considered necessary (167–68) and Lessing also demonstrates.

Joyce's schema for *Ulysses* provides the Homeric title for eighteen adventures and identifies the scene, major symbol, and technic for each and the hour, particular art, human organs, and colors for some (Gilbert 30). The schema implies Joyce's "heroic effort to give aesthetic order to the shellbits of our 'Humptydump world' immersed in the 'nightmare of history' " (Hayman 14).

The Golden Notebook, too, uses complex narrative strategies. Like *The Taming of the Shrew* or *Hamlet* with its play within a play or *The Canterbury Tales* with its stories within stories, *The Golden Notebook* reveals novels in novels, like Russian dolls. Anna Wulf, creatively blocked, fluctuates between "cannibalism" and either false sentiment or alienation, fears chaos, and projects her split self in four notebooks—black, red, yellow, and blue (Africa, communism, fiction, private life). Structurally, a section of "Free Women" in third-person-restricted point of view is followed by a section of each of Anna Wulf's four notebooks written about earlier times, in first person. (And the yellow notebook contains a novel about Ella, who writes a novel about a suicidal man.) The pattern repeats four times; then each notebook closes. In the inner "Golden Notebook" Anna reunifies her experience, writing in first person in a new notebook. We discover that "Free Women" is, after all, the novel Saul told her she must write to get a good look at her divided self. He gave her the first sentence: "The two women were alone in the London flat" (639, golden). *The Golden Notebook* concludes with a fifth section of "Free Women" in which the "fictional" Anna will become a social worker and Molly, her alter ego, will make a poor marriage. This outcome proves not to be the "reality." Writing her novel, which shows that sexually free women are not free of the desire for enduring love and fulfillment in all areas of life, implies that the "real" Anna, unblocked, becomes psychologically a free woman. We have been led to think that "Free Women" events result from notebook events—yet we may notice such discrepancies as the fact that Richard has three sons in "Free Women" but daughters in the notebooks and that Anna's former spouse is Willi in the black notebook and Max (not Marx or Marks) in the blue. Lessing tricks, then shocks and enlightens the reader, disclosing that "reality" and "appearance" may be deceptive.

Seeking objectivity, Eliot, Joyce, and Lessing use characters who are personae, masks. *The Waste Land,* for instance, may be the thoughts of some unidentified individual having a breakdown (like Eliot's), perhaps the bitter persona of the opening who dreads springtime and reawakened feeling. But the poem shifts voices and styles abruptly. We encounter other modern and ancient people, like figures of the tarot cards, who desire spiritual fulfillment, love, fertility—major motifs. In the mountains, thunder implies that rain is possible and tells people to give, sympathize, control. The fisherman who ought to be a Fisher King wonders, "Shall I at least set my lands in order?" (5.426). Or has he, like murderous Hieronymo, gone mad? A Hindu prayer beseeches the peace that passes understanding.

Leopold Bloom and Stephen Dedalus are both personae of Joyce as well as archetypal epic heroes or antiheroes. Bloom, half Jewish, half Irish, is treated as an outsider in Dublin. He is an outsider domestically as his wife turns to someone else for the sex Bloom has withheld since the death of their son, out of fear that fertility will lead to repeated tragedy. We trace the actions of this wandering Ulysses in Dublin and follow his thoughts, widespread in time and space, on 16 June 1904. They climax with his comic rescue of a modern Telemachus from a whorehouse and the police. Stephen Dedalus, a symbolic son to Bloom, briefly accepts the hospitality of his humane host, then departs, likely to become another self-exiled writer appreciative of the human comedy. Bloom concludes his day in bed, requesting Molly to bring him breakfast in the morning. Touchingly, because the modernist world is so fractured, it is in this Penelope's fragmented and sometimes muddled thoughts that Joyce's modern Ulysses regains his wife's love and achieves an image of wholeness.

Also an exile, Lessing's chief persona, Anna Wulf, has lived in Africa and England, married, had a child, divorced, published a novel, been a Communist, and undergone psychoanalysis. Though the battle of the sexes is Anna's major symbol of humankind's destructive will, she is also troubled by the evil in economics, politics, philosophy, science, and art; she has become blocked in creativity, like most people, "real" and "fictional," in *The Golden Notebook*. Perhaps as a result, Anna has a typical breakdown, but an exceptional breakthrough, believing that "the future might pour in a different shape" through "cracks" produced by neurotic conflict (473, blue). Archetypal images are used, like Nelson, Marx, Saul, Paul, Lear, Michael, Mary, Cinderella, Antigone, Electra. But Anna wants to separate in herself what is old and new. Refusing to drown, Narcissus-like, in the mind's pool of self-awareness, she compares herself mentally to other "real" and imagined people of the past, present, and future to discover how to live more creatively. Anna and Saul help each other believe both that energy can be used creatively and also that creative effort may just possibly make sense in their crazed, fragmented modern world.

For modernists like Lessing, Eliot, and Joyce, inner reality and psychological time, which Bergson called *durée*, are at least as important as outer reality and chronological time. The interior monologue, a stream of consciousness, discloses the flow of a person's thoughts; bits and pieces of imagery and information juxtaposed reveal his or her subjective reality. For example, each section of *The Waste Land* shows the thoughts of one troubled person or more; but the line "These fragments I have shored against my ruins" (5.431) may suggest that the entire poem is an interior monologue. The most famous example from *Ulysses* is the Penelope chapter, in which the reader participates in the stream-of-consciousness monologue of Molly Bloom as she falls asleep. But we also learn Stephen's thoughts in the Proteus chapter and those of Bloom in Calypso as he gets the cat's, Molly's, and his own breakfast. In *The Golden Notebook* Anna writes down many of her dream thoughts: Saul as a tiger, Mashopi, the Algerian soldier, a Chinese peasant. Dreams vivid as movies trouble her mind until new characters combine the strengths of "real" and "fictional" ones to act as models.

As another distancing technique, Eliot, Joyce, and Lessing achieve the appearance or parody of objectivity, on occasion, by mimicking drama. The distraught wife's questions, answered in thought by her husband in *The Waste Land* (2.111–38), anticipate Eugene O'Neill's *Strange Interlude*. Joyce, in the Circe episode, offers a stunning expressionist drama with stage notes. *The Golden Notebook* starts with a kind of stage note: "The two women were alone in the London flat," and the dialogue of "fictional" Anna and Molly suggests a scene in a play, though some exposition is provided—by the "real" Anna, author of "Free Women." Also, memoirs (Marie Larisch, *Waste Land*), diaries, or journals (Stephen Dedalus, *Portrait*; Anna Wulf, *GN*) may or may not be objective reality. Anna Wulf dislikes the "journalistic" writing that is popular and wants to write a philosophical novel. She does not succeed in "Free Women," where cynicism about her future belies her "real" achievement; but Lessing has written a philosophical novel in *The Golden Notebook*. Using modernist techniques, she tentatively justifies faith in humanism.

The "real" Anna accepts that human courage, at the root of life, is like the fertile blade of grass that rises after the holocaust. She quests for spiritual well-being like a modern Arthurian knight seeking a Holy Grail or a modern Ulysses going home. In "Free Women" "fictional" Anna dreams she must walk across a desert—where there is no water—toward mountains (408), recalling *The Waste Land*. Moreover, conscious intertextuality suggests the interrelatedness of *The Golden Notebook* and *Ulysses*. Three times Joyce is mentioned in *The Golden Notebook*. Molly's parents glittered briefly in the groups hovering around Aldous Huxley, D. H. Lawrence, and Joyce (7). Novels such as *Finnegans Wake* make Anna worry about "the thinning of language against the density of our experience." Can language communicate truth if a work can be read as "parody, irony or seriously" (300, 302, red)? Anna Wulf tries to recount one day (like Joyce's Bloomsday) faithfully— including a reference to menstruation reminiscent of Bloom's famous defecation. Describing menstruation reminds her of the difficulty of telling the truth yet showing literary tact. When "Joyce described his man in the act of defecating, it was a shock, shocking. Though it was his intention to rob words of their power to shock" (340, blue). The problem of conveying truth through language bedevils Anna. Like Eliot and Joyce, she tries many styles and admits at last that "real experience can't be described" in words, but she finds art preserves forms and creates significant patterns (633–34, golden).

Playing "the game" of linking microcosm and macrocosm, Anna may remind us of Stephen Dedalus reading the flyleaf of his geography book (*Portrait* 15–16). As a modern woman, she, like Jewish Molly Jacobs, has a larger range of interests than Joyce's Molly Bloom does. Anna Freeman Wulf, whose given name means "grace," psychologically divorces herself from bestiality, choosing to become a truly free woman. *The Golden Notebook* exhibits what Fromm calls "the truth of Spinoza's statement that *intellectual* knowledge is conducive to change only inasmuch as it is also *affective* knowledge" (93) and Freud's postulate "that man can become aware of the very forces which act behind his back—and that in becoming aware of them he enlarges the realm of freedom and is able to transform himself from a helpless puppet moved by unconscious forces to a self-aware and free man who determines his own destiny" (Fromm 100).

Eliot's essay "Tradition and the Individual Talent" contends that artists should be valued by the way in which they add to the literary tradition from Homer to the present and alter it with their contributions (506–07). Although the critical stance is arguable, the great modernists have made significant offerings to this body of work. *The Waste Land* is perhaps the most famous poem of the century because Eliot found such challenging metaphor, form, and content to compare the present with the past in a desperate quest for faith. In *Ulysses*, a comic novel, Joyce estimates a common man's potential to be a valid modern epic hero—or antihero. Lessing forces readers to reconsider the role of women and men in all art and history when she shows twentieth-century women are the equals of men in their need for self-integration and their concern to improve life; together, women and men must struggle to survive and to create a better era. For teachers who are like Lessing's boulder pushers, *The Golden Notebook* is a remarkable modernist touchstone of faith in humanism. Dropped into the pool of our students' awareness, it may even be an alchemist's stone.

A SPECTRUM OF CLASSROOMS

A Sixties Book for All Seasons

Joseph Hynes

A quarter of a century ago, when *The Golden Notebook* was quite new and when only reviewers and other "specialists" were talking about it, I read it out of duty. I had initiated a two-term graduate course in contemporary British fiction, under which label I meant to include important British, Irish, and Commonwealth writers of fiction who followed the modernist generation of Joyce, Woolf, Forster, and Lawrence. I started this course at Oregon because it seemed to me then, as it seems to me even more clearly now, that formal, systematic, curricular recognition of British literature since the late 1930s is virtually nonexistent in departments of English and is decidedly minimal amid the scores of exotic specialties offered on the annual MLA menu in December.

In any case, I read the book in the mid-sixties and reacted initially just as most of my students have reacted since those days. I knew that this was a serious and substantial work, and I suspected that it might even be a great book; but I had no very clear idea of the principle of its unity. It seemed to me a collection of false starts, arbitrarily reproduced, unaccountably repetitious, and anticlimactic at its close. In selecting it for the second term of my chronologically arranged course, I was moved not only by my hunch that here was a book worth studying but by the recognition—which I shared with the class of ten or fifteen students—that I was working with no profes-

sional advantage here. The students probably didn't believe me, but I meant
it when I told them that we were all going into this cave together and that
I had neither string nor flashlight.

In that course and in the same course for the next six or seven years, we
usually spent much time during our four or five sessions on this novel in
discussing isolated topics. Everyone was conscious of the cold war in those
days, for example, and the decade was also filled with "I-thou" sentiment.
Some students accordingly chose to write papers on Lessing and relevant
modern philosophers, or on Lessing and postwar liberal disillusionment.
Obviously *The Golden Notebook* invites thoughtful exploration of such topics.
So far, so good.

Then in the late sixties and early seventies feminism and the sexual revolution bore down hard, and predictably the students' attention moved from
East-West politics and I-thou involvement, and even from a certain emphasis
on Freudian versus Jungian analysis, to a much closer concern with sexual
politics and women's rights. As topics go, this one is decidedly important
to *The Golden Notebook* and the contemporary world. Of equal prominence
at this time was the broader topic of social justice—for workers, South African
blacks, and all underprivileged persons in addition to women as a specific
category.

These were some of the issues that readily lured students into the book
and provided them with items to chew on. As the years proceeded, however,
and while I was learning a good deal about such topics, I continued to feel
uneasy because *The Golden Notebook* still didn't add up for me and I therefore could not present it to the students as an intelligible whole. Then in
1970 or 1971 I decided that after the class had had its say about the usual
issues and problems, I would ask them why we were not paying more
attention to the book as a work of art, as we would look at other works well
known to English majors. I pointed out that we could all probably write
intelligent and convincing essays on the symmetry, integrity, or aesthetic
design of such works as *Tom Jones, Middlemarch,* and *The Ambassadors*
but that we all seemed stymied in our efforts to take the same approach to
The Golden Notebook. Although I did not say so to the class, I had reached
a point in my own study of this book where I was ready to put it aside, to
drop it from the course, if I could not crack it and discern its overall shape.
As the bibliographical note in my eventual essay suggests, the academic
community in those early days of critical attention to the book was writing
the same kinds of topical and thematic essays favored by my classes. Something more, something bigger, was called for.

My discomfort, I should perhaps emphasize, arose not because of anything
we were all saying about the various topics we had addressed and not because
I doubted the validity of locating Lessing more precisely among particular

psychologists, political parties, social activists, or feminists. Rather, I was bothered because of the disparateness of our collective perennial ventures. To date we had not succeeded in relating these strands and the papers written about them to each other. Lessing's overarching achievement was nowhere in our sight.

So I reverted to square one, or at least I tried to imagine what square one might have been. Specifically, I tried to imagine how to find and thereafter state what could have been Lessing's question in the first place. I tried to put myself in her shoes and to figure out what artistic problem she had set out to solve. Putting the quest in these terms implied subjugating to secondary status all the other issues discussed so far. That is, I wanted to find out what overriding problem Lessing had posed for herself, which, in the solving, would find all other problems fitting in as examples and details of that main problem's complexities and ramifications.

To clarify this obviously murky task, I got the students thinking about other literature that they had been exposed to in their careers. We had all discovered that knowing the shapes and structures of traditional English fictional classics gave us no help in focusing on *The Golden Notebook*. For this reason I asked them (and myself) to think of what Joyce was trying to achieve with *Ulysses* that was widely unintelligible in the 1920s but that is fairly well agreed on and understood today. The use of Homer gives *Ulysses* shape, we saw, and in fact *The Odyssey* is at least as much of a negative example and contrast as it is a positive shaping entity. What we needed was to discover some device analogous to Joyce's use of Homer, a device or system that would light up Lessing's work for us.

At this point I suggested that we might take a next step by lining up Lessing's book in the company of the other books we had been reading for two terms. At one extreme were fairly traditional realistic works of pre-modernism, such as Elizabeth Bowen's *Death of the Heart*, Evelyn Waugh's *Vile Bodies* and *Brideshead Revisited*, Graham Greene's *Brighton Rock*, Joyce Cary's *Herself Surprised*, and Anthony Powell's *Question of Upbringing*. In the middle range—different but readily decipherable by the class —were beautifully strange and wonderful works such as Henry Green's *Loving*, Iris Murdoch's *Severed Head*, and Muriel Spark's *Memento Mori*, books that are not in the nineteenth-century realistic tradition altogether but books whose differences from that tradition can be discerned and accommodated with some struggle. At the other extreme, finally, were Lawrence Durrell's *Alexandria Quartet*, Flann O'Brien's *At Swim-Two-Birds*, and John Fowles's *French Lieutenant's Woman*.

Setting things out in this fashion told us a good bit about both traditional and experimental strains in British fiction since the late 1930s. Moreover, we also began to see why we were having trouble finding a place for *The*

Golden Notebook. On the one hand, Anna Wulf was regularly insisting on her refusal to write anything but the big, epical, socially realistic novel modeled on *War and Peace* and *Buddenbrooks.* On the other hand, the volume we read is a record of failures to write that kind of book in the middle of the twentieth century, as well as a refusal to write such books as Durrell, O'Brien, and Fowles had written. Not only does Anna Wulf oppose commercial exploitation of what is possible in fiction, but she also requires of herself—as Tolstoy and Mann presumably required of themselves in their different times—a work that embodies all the truths known to the author; a thing of beauty that does not stand apart from the world that gives rise to it or exist in spite of or because of that world but, rather, that is the incarnation of that world as known to the author grossly and minutely. The art sought by Wulf-Lessing is the kind that supposedly gave rise to the great works of fictional realism. Lessing, like Anna Wulf, was trying to fashion a *premodernist* work, trying to revert to an art that the Joyce-Woolf group had abandoned as hopeless perhaps two generations before Lessing. Thus it would be as impossible, we saw, to try to fit Lessing's book into our third category as to fit it into our first. *The Golden Notebook,* that is, cannot be read as one reads Bowen's or Waugh's books, nor can it be read as straight or fellow-travelling psychological relativism or metafiction, like Durrell's, O'Brien's, or Fowles's books. Relativism and the ingenious aesthetic game playing and web constructing out of the metafictionist's innards are not for Lessing. Seeing her book in the context of her contemporaries' work makes clear that she is driven by the realist's aims as surely in *The Golden Notebook* as in all her books before and after this one—including *The Four-Gated City, Briefing for a Descent into Hell,* and the space fictions. Doris Lessing believes that objective truth exists, that it can be known, and that the writer's task is to find a way to embody it. And in *The Golden Notebook,* her most ambitious single volume, she tried heroically and impossibly to write all the truth known to her.

Getting myself and the students to this point, of course, was not a solution to the problem, but it did generate some different kinds of research papers. All the while I was blathering on about the shape of the work, I faced a new difficulty: that of persuading all of us that such talk was not in fact a dodging into safety and away from "relevance" staring at us from all the other oft-treated topical perches. I tried to convince all of us that, just as keeping in mind Joyce's use of *The Odyssey* certainly did not preclude our acute awareness of Anglo-Irish politics, modern sexual psychology, Irish anti-Semitism, or one distinct brand of cultural Catholicism, so our focusing on design could even heighten the significance of the several topics customarily seized on. The forest hardly existed without trees, I bravely whistled.

A number of students in the next couple of years worked on this lead in their papers, and at the same time I was busily making charts, lists, and diagrams and filling arrow-covered and cross-referenced pages, all in the hope of finding "the figure in the carpet." Anyone who has ever draped a room with summations of a life's notes while cramming for doctoral comprehensives will know what I mean. The difference between me and the examinee, however, was that I was not remembering history but searching for pattern.

The graphics helped. Sometime in 1972 the colors and personae and narrative points of view came together, and I wrote a first draft of "The Construction of *The Golden Notebook*." A couple of drafts later I sent it out and the *Iowa Review* published it in 1973. While I was waiting for its appearance, ironically, *Contemporary Literature* published its 1973 issue on Lessing, and I was pleased to see both that John Carey had entertained the same questions that had plagued me and my students over the years and that his essay and mine were not interchangeable.

Metaphorically speaking, my essay makes the case for *The Golden Notebook* as a five-layered sandwich. The five chapters of "Free Women" are slices of bread, between each two pieces of which appear sizable portions of multicolored delicatessen (black, red, yellow, blue, golden). Moreover, the "Free Women" segments postdate and in an important sense emerge from the multicolored segments. This temporal arrangement of an intense spiritual struggle is Lessing's way of conveying her awareness of levels of creativity at work in establishing several Annas. More precisely, the political, sexual, authorial Annas of the colored books are selectively arranged in four parts per color and placed, with the Anna of the small golden notebook, in chronological sequence between consecutive chapters of "Free Women." This placing function in turn is achieved by an Anna-editor who writes from time to time within square brackets about the varying handwriting in the notebooks. Beyond this editing Anna we find Doris Lessing, whose imagination encompasses the whole five-layered sandwich and the editor. And of course beyond Lessing lies the reader, whose imaginative effort ensures that *The Golden Notebook* continues to expand for everyone who enters into its moral, emotional complexity.

My contention is that Anna Wulf and Doris Lessing inevitably fail in their attempt to make a unity of all life and art. At the same time, however, the determination to create a pattern that will produce both the drab, well-made "Free Women" *and* the intense, fragmented notebook segments shows Anna's and Lessing's refusal *simply* to fail. The decision was clearly, complicatedly, to merge failure with the refusal to give up the quest. Failure becomes a kind of success.

Since that time I have taught *The Golden Notebook* regularly to my graduate students and have also taught it four or five times to my junior and senior classes in twentieth-century literature. This is a popular three-term course of several sections, each of about fifty students, half of them not English majors. By the time I tried the book among these undergraduates I had published the essay and tried it on a few more groups of graduate students. As the years have gone by, both graduates and undergraduates seem to appreciate this novel more, and I think their more appreciative reading is due in part to my having come to terms with the book's structure and meaning. My reading, like any other, is hardly the last word, but I remain convinced that some such structural and ontological framework is essential if readers are to avoid impressionism and isolated focus on whatever topic happens to strike their fancy. Obviously I am aware of the danger of forcing students to see things my way and to write party-line papers. This, however, is a perennial danger and one worth risking if the alternative is random insight into one or another of the book's themes.

In the fourteen years since my essay appeared, I have of course watched the students come to take South African politics for granted, almost ignore the "Red menace," assume the rightness of women's fight for equality, and at the same time note that Lessing has fallen out of favor with many feminists because (I believe) she refuses to simplify this issue or to let it blind her to the rest of the world. I have also seen students grow enthusiastic over metafiction and postmodernism, leave literature and elope with theory, and then become disillusioned with theory. I rehearse this overgeneralized story of the past twenty years of literary study because I want to make the point that this history has persuaded me thus far that my essay was motivated by the right impulse. As I said in my essay and as I continue to believe, *The Golden Notebook* remains an important and vital book because the imagination and intelligence that put it together in the first place do not depend on a reader's empathy for particular current events. Rather, Lessing's art causes the novel to endure just as Gustave Flaubert's art keeps *Madame Bovary* in the curriculum and Jane Austen's art prevents our discarding *Emma*.

Students, like some professional critics, have predictably sniped at such outbursts as those in the preceding paragraph. Not only the no-nonsense business major, but the dedicated literature student, has asked me whether I am advocating art for art's sake. My response is that I honestly don't know what art for art's sake could possibly be and that what I am pushing them to see is art for life's sake. This somewhat pretentious retort allows me to come down to earth, to cite all the very details of *The Golden Notebook* that they fear I have forgotten, and to conclude that all those details must be accounted for and envisioned and valued together as well as (not instead of) separately if we are to see what Lessing and Anna were setting out to do and if we are to see the human importance of trying against all odds to get all of oneself into a book.

The irony is that before 1973 I felt at one with students in a quest for pattern, when we were all working hard on particulars, while since 1973 the very fact that I now have posited a structural framework often arouses students' skepticism and even antagonism because they are inclined to suppose that I wouldn't be going on in this fashion about art and form and design if I really cared about the world we live in. Inevitably I try to show the students that positing such a dichotomy is crucial to seeing and feeling Anna Wulf's problem. I think the dichotomy unfair to me as a critic, and that sense of unfairness helps me—and perhaps my students—to experience Anna's frustration at being unable to capture all experience and make it into a work of beauty. Form ought to *be* content, not merely to buttress it.

The next time I teach *The Golden Notebook* I will take along the present volume of essays. When the students then insist that I must choose between involvement and detachment, I will point to the table of contents. I will remark that, although fifteen of seventeen contributors are women, for instance, the variety of critical approaches taken and developed in the past twenty-five years proves that serious interest in *The Golden Notebook* is assuredly not limited to the province of scholars using feminist critical tools. All students of Lessing have profited from the burst of critical energy expended on Lessing's book. At the same time, my experience in the classroom continues to show that, however eclectic one's teaching of *The Golden Notebook*, any critical, social, theoretical, moral, or political approach or complex of approaches can and must be accommodated within some such framework as I have provided. An approach that cannot be accommodated demands the adjusting, not the discarding, of the framework. Second-floor vistas, hallways, doors, and windows may be appreciated, but it would be folly to forget the building that makes them possible even as they are the particulars that enable us to speak appreciatively of the building. Finally, I will simply restate my own theme that each of these approaches is imaginative, informative, and worthwhile and that each implies the question, What does this reading say about the *whole* of *The Golden Notebook*? Eventually and in the long run any serious reader must ask that question of any book read and must attempt to supply an answer. The trouble arising from the answer is preferable to the trouble encountered before the existence of that answer. Let us have more answers.

The Golden Notebook in an Introductory Women's Studies Course

Roberta Rubenstein

Those of us who love and admire Doris Lessing's rich, multifaceted masterpiece *The Golden Notebook* may not always anticipate the difficulties it raises in the classroom. The age and gender of the student, the reader's (and the teacher's) assumptions about male-female relationships, the historical distance from the time period in which Lessing's novel is set, and the associations imposed by the book's relation to other works in a given course obviously affect students' understanding of this complex, resonant narrative. Having taught *The Golden Notebook* in several graduate seminars on modern fiction, in undergraduate courses on experimental fiction and on literature focusing on women, and in an introductory women's studies course, I can say that the last context posed the greatest challenges because students came to the course with the least experience as readers of imaginative narrative. As a result, from that course I probably learned most about the problems and rewards of teaching the novel.

The introductory women's studies course I discuss here was a new one, developed (by me in collaboration with another colleague) and being taught for the first time as a requirement for students minoring in women's studies—of whom there were only a few in the first years of the women's studies program on my campus. Others took the course as an elective. Of the nearly thirty students who enrolled in it, all were women, mostly between the ages of eighteen and twenty-five. Many of them were freshmen and sophomores, often still undecided about the direction of their academic studies; they tended toward majors in business or the social sciences.

On the basis of what had preceded *The Golden Notebook* in the syllabus (different theoretical or descriptive approaches to the social construction of gender), students assumed that there was a body of information for them to master, at which point they would understand what the novel, like the previous readings, had to say about such subjects as gender roles and the historical status of women. In the shift to engagement with imaginative narrative, they were being asked to encompass a more complicated discovery, a mode of knowledge that depends on comprehension not only of structure and content but of feeling and one that does not emerge until the student enters into and completes the process of reading, talking, and writing about Anna Wulf in her diverse self-representations.

Most of the students in the class were inexperienced both as literary readers and as young women. Many of them admitted that they felt too young to identify with Anna's self-divisions as mother, lover, writer, and political activist. Looking for ways to comprehend *The Golden Notebook* in terms of gender issues and women's choices, they were mystified not only by what seemed to them an unnecessarily cumbersome structure but by some of the dimensions of Anna Wulf's predicament. Since the first 150 pages of the novel embrace Anna's own context setting—the initial segments of the black and red notebooks illuminating her African experiences, her earlier writing, and her political self-searchings—it is quite some time before readers looking for "women's issues" find dimensions of the narrative that fulfill their expectations in recognizable ways. Initially, students wondered what this book was doing in a women's studies course in the first place.

In trying to address this response, I discovered a generation gap that I had not experienced in teaching *The Golden Notebook* in more strictly literary contexts. (In literature courses, Lessing's novel is typically contextualized by other literary works that provide thematic, structural, historical, or ideological connections.) Anna Wulf "lives through" the late fifties—a time close to the period that many of us who teach *The Golden Notebook* also lived through and that shaped our own identities: the era of the civil rights movement, the Vietnam war, campus unrest, and, of course, the women's liberation movement. Lessing chided her earliest readers for thinking that the novel was about women's liberation and the "sex war" rather than, as she insisted in her 1972 introduction to *The Golden Notebook*, "a book which would make its own comment, a wordless statement: to talk through the way it was shaped" (xiv). As she also observed, "This book was written as if the attitudes that have been created by the Women's Liberation movements already existed. . . . If it were coming out now for the first time it might be read, and not merely reacted to" (ix–x). Despite Lessing's objections, many of us nonetheless found in Anna a hero of our time and in *The Golden Notebook* a central text that articulated our experiences as women. Ironically, it may be harder for young women in college now, reading rather than "reacting to" the novel, to see as central the gender issues that readers twenty years ago saw to the exclusion of other dimensions of the narrative.

Thus, one challenge that some teachers of *The Golden Notebook* share with Doris Lessing's protagonist is the necessity to come to terms with nostalgia: not only Anna Wulf's but our own. Most of the students in my women's studies class were not even born until after the critical years that link Anna with those of us who came of age, either chronologically or politically, about the time Lessing's novel was published. Though the age gap between professor and students sometimes affects other kinds of college classes, the impact was exacerbated in this women's studies course because the subject matter so directly affected students' perceptions of their own lives as women. Initially (and sometimes even ultimately) they tended to see Lessing's novel as dated, Anna Wulf's dilemmas as part of past history. Anna's problems were problems of her time, not of ours—or, I should say, of theirs, since many students perceive their female professors as closer in age and experience to Anna than to themselves. Anna, as a contemporary of their mothers and teachers, faced problems that (they naively assumed) are no longer concerns for women of their generation in the eighties. (This is a difficulty that many teachers of introductory women's studies courses face: the unconsidered attitude of many college students today—male as well as female—who see women as doctors, lawyers, network news anchors, and astronauts and assume that all the issues of social and gender equality have been adequately solved.) In responding to the students' historical short-sightedness, I focused on the slow pace of change in women's lives (including their mothers'); other course readings also supported this fact.

The well-known parable of the five blind men and the elephant (a Sufi tale that Doris Lessing herself has cited) could be read as analogous to the experience of teaching *The Golden Notebook*. Students "touch," or engage with, the text from different perspectives and backgrounds; one must guide the student who feels only the skin or the trunk (and draws conclusions accordingly)—the "story" of a sexually and emotionally frustrated woman, or of a single mother, or of a blocked writer—to discover the tail/tale, so to speak. A number of students, indeed feeling their way blindly through the narrative, inevitably became impatient with Lessing and with Anna Wulf (and with me).

Students of literature who have experience with narrative forms—even if they have never read an experimental novel—have interpretive skills to bring to bear on a novel in which chronology, continuity, realism, and point of view are deliberately scrambled. Readers with little interpretive context, however, expect the customary handles of stable character portraits, plot, and "theme." My untrained students found that the unconventional structure of *The Golden Notebook* got in the way of their making sense of Anna Wulf as a character. They resisted my argument that the sequence of notebooks, the apparent disorganization and disruption of chronology, the shifts in point of view and multiplicity of characters, and the remorseless self-examination by its central consciousness were essential elements rather than obstacles to their understanding of Anna Wulf's experiences and of the novel as a whole. Floundering in the narrative formlessness, they wanted to be told what was "important" in the vast accumulation of detail; they longed for something that would reduce their bewilderment, a key that would unlock the door to comprehension without their having to earn it by participating fully in the novel's process.

Moreover, because the students' other courses typically had a lecture rather than a discussion format, I found that I had to work against their expectation that I would tell them what to think about the assigned readings—including the novels—before they had formulated their own ideas. Yet, as I eventually discovered, neither the syllabus nor I had adequately prepared them for the shift in expectation and for the kind of response required for reading and understanding imaginative literature. To my mind, this is the fundamental challenge in teaching *The Golden Notebook*, regardless of the course context: to guide students into that process without giving it all away in advance; to enable them to accept the sense of dislocation, entering into Anna's disaffection and her radically disintegrating mental and emotional experiences, living inside her mind as she moves from destructive fragmentation and compartmentalization to at least a qualified recognition (depending on how one reads the ending) of synthesis and recovery.

Thus, it was necessary for me to help students anticipate what to expect in structural, thematic, and historical terms. Yet, because I felt that they needed to come to terms with *The Golden Notebook* as a whole before they could isolate what the novel might have to say about "women's issues" and also because I did not want to oversimplify the text in the process of making it more accessible, I tried to assist them by suggesting questions to try to answer as they read, starting with simple and general ones and moving toward more probing ones. The following questions were developed for students to use in preparing for class discussions:

What do you discover about Anna Wulf in each section? What does Anna discover about herself?

What ideas and concerns shape each segment?

Why is the novel organized in this way? What is the function or governing preoccupation of each notebook? of the "Free Women" sections? What does "free women" mean?

What views does the novel present about women? about men? about men and women together?

How are Anna's past experiences as a young woman in southern Africa related to other aspects of her experience?

How is Anna's situation as a single woman and mother related to other aspects of her experience?

How are Anna's concerns as an artist related to other aspects of her experience?

How are Anna's political concerns related to other aspects of her experience?

What are some of the central and recurrent images of the novel? What is their significance?

What is the "reality" of Anna Wulf's experiences? Does she know this? Can we know this? What is the relation between "truth" and "fact" in the narrative? between "truth" and "invention"?

Is Anna "mad"? If so, what does this mean?

Who is Anna Wulf? Has she changed by the end of the novel? If so, how?

What do you have in common with Anna Wulf?
How do you understand the ending of the novel?
What is *The Golden Notebook* about, finally?

Only when students had penetrated much further into what initially seemed an impenetrable text did they begin to make sense of Anna Wulf's personality and her inner crisis—and of what Lessing might have to say on the subject of women. Other problems inevitably arose (but at least they reflected students' engagement with the text): for example, an intense irritation with Anna's self-destructive, masochistic attachments to men unworthy of her. As students saw it, none of the male characters depicted in the novel had any positive characteristics; they were all sadistic, emotionally parasitic, self-serving, and arrogant—no wonder Anna was miserable and crazy. Wondering whether the implication was that men were rotten or that Anna was attracted to rotten men, some of the women felt that either alternative described a set of relations between the sexes more cynical and destructive than they were prepared to accept; they felt that Lessing had exaggerated the negative dimension beyond credibility. Confident that heterosexual relationships had improved in the twenty-five years since the publication of *The Golden Notebook*, they resisted some of the implications of Anna's conflicts among desire, need, intimacy, maternal responsibility, artistic integrity, political conviction, and personal independence. Yet, as they explored her process of self-discovery and partial recovery, they began to see more clearly the social, sexual, and psychological difficulties besetting a "free woman."

The best students grasped that Anna Wulf's inner crisis mirrors a world that was in chaos then and, although the superficial lineaments of chaos may have changed somewhat, is no less so today. The dilemmas that Anna confronts—her struggle to be not only a whole self but a whole woman in a world where female identity is both shaped and undermined by attitudes toward sexuality, emotional needs, conflicts between nurturance and career, and political-geopolitical madness—spoke to students as well, resonating with questions they recognized as part of their own reality.

My experience with teaching *The Golden Notebook* to female non–English major undergraduates thus revealed certain problems, ranging from the generation gap and the historical, political, and literary naïveté of traditional undergraduate women to the critical ways in which course context molds expectation and response. Students in a women's studies course expect gender to be the primary subject regardless of the text. Obviously this subject can be explored through imaginative literature as well as through descriptive and theoretical social science texts. Indeed, as a professor of literature I had felt that Lessing's novel was singularly important in this very context—but I had underestimated the way in which structural complexity impeded that discovery for many students. Moreover, in an introductory course it is difficult to accomplish interdisciplinary breadth as well as literary depth.

I have concluded that *The Golden Notebook* may not be the best novel to achieve the goals of an introductory women's studies course, although some women in my class found it a very valuable text for identifying—and identifying with—the emotional and social circumstances confronting "free women." In subsequent offerings of the course, I substituted Lessing's *Marriages between Zones Three, Four and Five*—in which gender stereotypes are clearly foregrounded—with great success. I have also increased the proportion of literary works in the course, including more short stories and several novels such as Zora Neale Hurston's *Their Eyes Were Watching God*, Charlotte Perkins Gilman's *Herland*, or Toni Morrison's *Bluest Eye*—all accessible and provocative literary works that complement the social science readings in the syllabus.

For those who are considering using *The Golden Notebook* in a women's studies introductory course, my experience suggests that an interrogative mode is useful for inexperienced readers. Through questions that address both structural and thematic matters, students can approach the complexities of the text as well as their own confusion as readers. The questions given in this essay emerged in response to the needs of my class; other teachers will undoubtedly formulate different ones. In addition, one can share with students some understanding of the historical and psychological contexts that illuminate the process of reading Lessing's narrative through the lens of gender. (Simone de Beauvoir's *Second Sex* is particularly instructive for this purpose.)

Women's studies courses enable students to understand women's historical and contemporary situations. In order for these students to comprehend Anna Wulf's experiences as well as the unique characteristics of the narrative structure through which they are represented, we as teachers need to help them discover that Lessing's unconventional forms and techniques are not irrelevant aspects of the novel. If we can successfully establish those questions and contexts, we can enable students to participate imaginatively in one of the most profound explorations of a woman's complex consciousness that exists in fiction.

The Golden Notebook:
In Whose or What Great Tradition?

Claire Sprague

When the concept of tradition is applied to the English novel, F. R. Leavis is the critic most likely to be invoked. Leavis's Great Tradition, more open than T. S. Eliot's would-be royalist, classicist, Anglo-Catholic tradition, admitted two women, Jane Austen and George Eliot; two foreigners, Henry James and Joseph Conrad; and one lower-middle-class male, D. H. Lawrence. Doris Lessing, female and foreign and emphatically not upper-class, sits uneasily—if at all—within the Leavis or any English tradition. When she herself played the game of creating a tradition in the 1950s, she defined herself as more European than English, closer to her favorite Russian and French novelists, Tolstoy and Stendhal, than to Dickens, Eliot, or Hardy. In fact, she wrote about nineteenth-century novels in ways that suggested her own desire to be ranked as the English Tolstoy rather than the English Eliot. We are all familiar with her statement in "The Small Personal Voice" (1957): "For me the highest point of literature was the novel of the nineteenth century, the work of Tolstoy, Stendhal, Dostoevsky, Balzac, Turgenev, Chekhov" (*Small Personal Voice* 4). No English-born novelist could have made such a list without mentioning a single English writer. This list, one of the many modes through which Lessing deliberately distances herself from English tradition, implicitly defines that tradition as insular and unusable in the post–World War II period.

In her 1971 introduction to *The Golden Notebook* Lessing places "the book . . . more in the European tradition than the English tradition of the novel" (xiv). George Eliot, here omitted and nowhere a central figure in Lessing's "usable past" (Brooks), appears earlier in the preface, in effect as an example of the failure of the English novel to describe "the intellectual and moral climate of a hundred years ago, in the middle of the last century, in Britain, in the way Tolstoy did it for Russia, Stendhal for France" (x). Eliot, rated "good as far as she goes" (xi), fails to write the big representative book of her time that Lessing wished to write for hers. We can infer that Lessing would rather have written *War and Peace* than *Middlemarch* and would disagree with Leavis, who claimed for Eliot's "best work . . . a Tolstoyan depth and reality" (125).

Without entering into the range of questions that can and should be asked about the origin, development, and etiology of literary tradition(s), let us agree that Lessing forces her readers to break out of a merely national into a transnational theater. She is, in short, a writer who forces a comparative approach on us in rather special ways at a time when comparativists are themselves enlarging their own previously "Continentalist" approach to include women and non-Western literatures (M. L. Pratt 35; see also Rose).

For Reinhold Grimm, "the password everywhere in letters" is " 'comparability unlimited' " (29) rather than "Eurocentric pieties about the nature of 'man' " (Culler 30). As a white female African writing in English, Lessing takes the world as her country. As such she can be compared with English or other nationals, white or not, female or not. When I have paired Lessing with Eliot, department traditionalists permitted Lessing to be tacked on to a recognized "great" like Eliot. Putting Lessing and Lawrence together, as I have also done, met with greater resistance. When that resistance goes (and it is not far away, as this volume testifies) and *The Golden Notebook* is fully embalmed as a classic, we may have more to worry about.

There is never enough time. I have never had the luxury some colleagues have had of devoting a course solely to *Middlemarch* and *The Golden Notebook*. These long, dense works are only two among other works by these authors or others in my courses, although I speak here as though they are the only two.

Few of my students in the last two or three years have heard of or read Lessing. I have taught *The Golden Notebook* on the undergraduate and graduate level, in standard courses on contemporary English literature, in women's studies courses, and in special colloquiums on topics like Eliot and Lessing, Lessing and Lawrence, and the double in literature. It is not easy for undergraduates, majors as well as nonmajors, to be drawn into the novel's "intimidating comprehensiveness" (Marovitz uses this phrase for *Moby-Dick* [56]). The same "intimidating comprehensiveness" characterizes *Middlemarch*. One way I try to overcome the overwhelming nature of these novels is to break assignments up into manageable parts. I subdivide and paginate the notebooks sections to correlate with the "Free Women" 1, 2, 3, 4, 5 sections and always speak of the notebooks by number, as black 1, 2, 3, 4; red 1, 2, 3, 4; and so on. I spend a good deal of time on the opening pages and often flip to the very last line of the novel, "The two women kissed and separated." In this elegant whodunit, the last line doesn't tell all, but it does establish a link between the beginning and the end and thus inevitably raises the question of shape in the novel.

We talk about the global politics of the 1950s as much or as little as we talk about provincial politics on the eve of the Reform Bill of 1832. For the generation of the 1980s, politics is not generally a passionate pursuit. But the passion that informs the novels, the committedness that is Lessing's and Eliot's, attracts students. The multiple and intersecting chronologies of *The Golden Notebook* interest students a great deal as part of the general proposition that the novel "does not make a monolithic proposition about reality" (to use Axelrod's description of *Moby-Dick* [68]). Sometimes I write out the parallel chronologies and show how the novel meets in the present time of the novel at its conclusion. Sometimes I use published diagrams (e.g., Hedin;

Kums; Mulkeen) as well as my own to clarify chronology, character, and politics. Once students perceive Anna as not necessarily the same person in each section, once they allow themselves to question "the old stable *ego* of the character" (Lawrence, qtd. in Leavis 24), their zest in proceeding increases exponentially. They want the inner "Golden Notebook" to be whole and beautiful, are disappointed when it isn't, but are able finally to recognize that incompleteness and contradiction can have an exhilaration impossible in the happy closures of nineteenth-century novels. The double or discrepant endings of blue 4 and "Free Women" 5, often confusing at first, finally become epiphany. As a radical restructuring of reality, the novel unsettles the novelistic expectations that most students still have.

The "network of parallels and contrasts" in *Middlemarch* (Harvey 11–12) has inexact analogues in *The Golden Notebook*. Eliot's characters are all self-evidently freestanding, not so Lessing's, yet parallels and contrasts are as much a feature of the later as well as the earlier novel. Both are dealing with multiple plots, multiple characters, and shifting points of view, although in very different ways. Both insist on the fluidity of character. Strikingly absent in the mid-twentieth-century novel is a viable community, one that brings to heel a communally recognized evil man like Bulstrode. There is no communal voice and no communal power in Lessing's novel. The outside world impinges only through headlines in newspapers. There can be no town meetings, no shoemakers, no parsons, no farmers, no storekeepers, no neighbors. Once in "Free Women" we hear a voice selling strawberries. That voice is exceptional. Perhaps that is why the group scenes in the Mashopi Hotel have such power, played as they are against the Boothbys and the Jacksons, the racist petty bourgeoisie and the black servant class. Lessing's stated desire to see the individual and the collective in dialectic interaction is played out on a very small scale. This reduction has a claustrophobic effect that global headlines do not alter.

Oddly, then, for fiction so often characterized as flat-footedly realist, Lessing's novel tends toward solipsism. Its multiple points of view, its many characters are spun entirely out of Anna's head. The characters often seem displaced parts of Anna's self or "manifestations of certain forces or principles" (Lifson 98; see also Rubenstein, *Novelistic Vision*; Sprague, *Rereading Doris Lessing*). In the inner "Golden Notebook," the image of montage, taken from film lingo, illustrates the permeability of personality. Under its power, conventions of time and space destruct, and women and men melt into a single female, a single male, even into a single entity like the figure of Tiresias in *The Waste Land* (Sprague, *Rereading Doris Lessing* 24, 60, 77). This kind of permeability of personality is not a feature of Eliot's novel, for Eliot's characters retain their "realistic" or "hard edge" dimensions, their usual "frames." (See Draine, *Substance*, ch. 7, for the concept of breaking frames.)

One of the richest areas for comparative discussion—there are so many —is, of course, the portrayal of women together with men before, during, after, and outside marriage. Eliot explodes the earlier marriage plot in her own way. (It simply doesn't exist in *The Golden Notebook*.) Dorothea's two marriages represent a radical departure from other nineteenth-century novels. That very odd couple, Dorothea Brooke and Anna Wulf, inevitably provokes many comparative questions about women, marriage, and vocation. Lessing's gallery—the multiple Annas, Molly, Ella, Julia, Maryrose, Marion, Mrs. Marks (Mother Sugar)—are as rich in parallels and contrasts as Eliot's gallery—Dorothea, Celia, Rosamond, Mary, the actress Laure, Mrs. Bulstrode, Mrs. Garth. Lessing's men—Paul Blackenhurst, Richard, Tommy, Michael, Paul Tanner, DeSilva, Saul Green—are not so various or given such meticulous contexts as are Lydgate, Casaubon, Mr. Brooke, Will, Chettam, and Bulstrode, but this listing suggests the passion for networks both writers share.

Both writers also share a passion for seeing double. Their novels open with two women—Dorothea and Celia, Anna and Molly—and explore female friendships in unusually rich ways. However, the Dorothea-Rosamond interaction in *Middlemarch* has no counterpart in *The Golden Notebook*. Lessing's women are more equal; they almost never relate with antagonism or volatility. That kind of interaction is reserved for Anna's relations with men. Nevertheless, contrast and contraries pattern both novels. The juxtaposition of "Free Women" to the notebooks is, for example, a major contrast in *The Golden Notebook*; all the titles of the eight books in *Middlemarch* save the first juxtapose two persons or events.

Eliot's descriptions of the Rosamond-Lydgate marriage as "a yoked loneliness" (462) and of Dorothea's as painfully unfree have extraordinary ironic echoes for the "free women" in Lessing's novel. Dorothea's "perfect liberty of misjudgment" (47), once reserved for upper-class women like herself, Gwendolen Harleth, or Isabel Archer, is now equally available to middle- and lower-class women like Anna Wulf or Martha Quest. The issue of what it means for a woman to be free is central to both novels. The issue of vocation, intimately connected with the issue of greatness for women, is also at the heart of both novels.

"The moment of vocation" Lydgate experiences (98) is wholly denied to Dorothea. But Anna, although denied the epiphanic "moment," is not denied the vocation itself. However blocked, agonized, skeptical, or ambiguous Anna is about her vocation, she is a writer. (The earnings from her first novel are still coming in and are still enough to live on.) As a writer, she belongs to a particularly privileged male realm, one forbidden to Eliot's fictional women and imagined for only two of Lessing's many fictional women (Anna Wulf and Jane Somers).

To place a professional woman writer at the center of a novel was and continues to be an act of imaginative and political daring. It is also daring to subvert, as the novel does, the commonly held proposition that women are by nature nonviolent. It can, in fact, be said that Anna's education is completed—in terms of the novel—when she internalizes the destructive principle she has for almost the entire novel insisted resides in men only. When Anna has worked away the complex disguises of dream to discover that she is the male/female dwarf, that she is cannibal as well as victim, she can dream her destruction dream "positively." This insight is the triumph of the notebook sections.

Whether or not nature "intended greatness for men" (*Middlemarch* 269), greatness as an ideal is undercut in both novels, which come down on the side of humbler pursuits. The energy and ambition of Casaubon, Lydgate, and Bulstrode are destroyed while caring modes are upheld in Will, Dorothea, Mary Garth, and Mrs. Bulstrode. The conclusions to both novels are muted, even elegiac. No Theresa or Antigone can flourish in our time; Anna, the Laure of *Middlemarch* transformed, chooses welfare work over writing. Yet Eliot insists that "the growing good of the world is partly dependent on unhistoric acts" (578). This is like Anna's preference for the concreteness of tomatoes and tea over abstraction; concretions are her hold on reality, her stay against madness. It is even more like Paul Tanner's image of himself and Anna as boulder pushers, as unspectacular servants of humanity. Lessing's title for her most well known essay, "The Small Personal Voice," inscribes in yet another way her version of the significance of "unhistoric acts," her skepticism about fame, language, art, relationships. Molly's husband is no Will Ladislaw; Anna doesn't marry at all. Lessing's voice is on one level more despairing, yet on another more exultant, for the Anna of blue 4 and the inner "Golden Notebook" wrote the novel in which another Anna decides to become a counselor.

This level, the metafictional level of *The Golden Notebook*, is unique. On this level, the novel is triumphant, although it infinitely problematizes, resisting "closure that it construes as enclosure" (Hite). "The undoing of hierarchy and containment" (Hite) is central to the feminist enterprise. Both *The Golden Notebook* and *Middlemarch*, written by women often highly critical of women and of protofeminist or feminist outlooks, nonetheless constantly undercut or struggle against "hierarchy and containment."

In pitting the image of the key (Casaubon, Lydgate) against the image of the web, Eliot focuses her rejection of an "acquisitive and reductive monism" characterized as male against female interconnection and complexity (Gilbert and Gubar 509; Haight xiv). The constant interleaving of texts in *The Golden Notebook*, the presentation of internally juxtaposed subtexts—novels in progress, newspaper clippings, parodies, film scripts, diaries, short stories —are Lessing's way of choosing web over key. The novel's insistence on the collaborative nature of art is another manifestation of its preference for web over key or ego.

The interleaving mode of the novel—even the neat narrative "Free Women" sections acquire force only when juxtaposed against the notebooks—can be perceived as collage rather than montage. A similar observation has been made about *Middlemarch*; it has been called "a bundle of stories loosely tied together" (Haight xv). These observations can sustain students who perceive the novel's structure as choppy or hard to follow. (They are right.) The novel's overall collage and occasionally montage structure delights film and art history majors. Other students see the book's structure as "its most interesting part" and argue that "Lessing's choice of narration(s) forms the meaning of the novel" (Caroline Loewald, student) or that "the formal aspects of the novel . . . mirror the content" (Debra Wachsberger, student).

Students also respond very positively to the concept of open-endedness. I insist on the novel as a demonstration of process, even though Anna and Molly sell out at the end of "Free Women" 5. Lessing defines their sellout as a sign of the times (*Small Personal Voice* 75). Like all "classics," *The Golden Notebook* is, therefore, paradoxically at once a period piece meticulously tied to its time and miraculously beyond it. The novel's public and sexual politics are very much of its time. Its homophobia, its acceptance of vaginal orgasm, "one of the male myths of the day" (Spilka 237), are two examples of its location in time, as are the specifics of its politics.

Lessing's comment in her preface, "I was learning as I wrote" (ix), is liberating for students. It tells them, as the novel tells them again and again, that process is all, that not everything has been done or written. "It keeps opening up," as one student put it. "The full book" is finally at once "all-inclusive and incomplete" (Hynes 104).

The comparative mode inevitably forces students and teachers to unsettle stabilities. It erodes the concept of tradition as something inexorably evolving in linear fashion. It doesn't destroy the idea of tradition, but it does place it in permanent question, making it provocative and protean. Like the newer emphases in evolutionary theory, tradition must be viewed as proceeding in time through punctuated leaps rather than through slow accretions over millennia. We are now in a punctuating period. "Comparability unlimited" has to be the password of our approach to *The Golden Notebook*. The Eliot-Lessing connection is alive and well and living in *The Golden Notebook*, although Lessing as critic has belittled or ignored it.

The Golden Notebook in a Graduate Seminar on Contemporary Experimental Fiction

Molly Hite

The class is called Postmodern Fiction, and it deals with those novelists and short story writers who are most commonly associated with the avant-garde of the post-1960 period. To call these writers postmodern, or indeed to call anything postmodern, is to enter into one of the grand disputes of twentieth-century studies (the dispute invariably rages throughout this class), but there does exist a relatively stable canon—or "precanon," to borrow Richard Ohmann's useful term—of works that fall under this inflammatory rubric, a list that is sanctioned by such disparate authorities as Larry McCaffery (247–564); John Barth, in his influential essays "The Literature of Exhaustion" (62–76) and "The Literature of Replenishment" (193–206); and the entire run of *Boundary 2: A Journal of Postmodern Literature* (in print since the mid-1970s). When I first taught the course in 1983, I was careful to invoke the authority of the precanon as a hedge against the theoretical vulnerability that is in many ways inherent in the term *postmodern*. I used fiction by nine writers, seven of them American (if you count Nabokov), one Irish (Beckett), one Argentinian (Borges, in translation). All the writers were men. The precanon of postmodernism is, after all, almost exclusively male, at least the way it is currently constituted.

For a number of reasons this situation bothered me, most significantly because it seemed to reflect a widespread cultural preconception that women somehow write "straight," aiming to "express themselves" in some vaguely unmediated way and thus eschewing structural and stylistic innovation. Such thinking not only tends to remove women from serious consideration (for example, by removing them from courses like mine) but tends to misrepresent the achievement of those women writers who in fact are experimenting with fictional structure and style. *The Golden Notebook* seemed to me a signal case in point, inasmuch as it has a long history of naturalizing readings—that is, readings that attempt to reconcile different levels of "reality" within the novel by invoking realist conventions, in particular the convention of frame story and imbedded "fiction." I regularly taught *The Golden Notebook* in my undergraduate course on twentieth-century women novelists, and the students regularly read it in terms of its representations of women's experience. How might a group of bright and critically up-to-date graduate students read it if it were presented within a context of radically experimental fiction?

When I taught Postmodern Fiction for the second time, in 1985, I had introduced a small but I hoped significant element of sexual difference into the syllabus. Graduate classes meet only once a week for approximately two hours. I had set up the weeks as follows:

Week 1   Introduction and discussion
Week 2   Saul Bellow, *Herzog*
Week 3   John Hawkes, *Second Skin*
Week 4   Margaret Atwood, *Lady Oracle*
Week 5   Vladimir Nabokov, *Pale Fire*
Weeks 6 and 7   Doris Lessing, *The Golden Notebook*
Week 8   Jorge Luis Borges, *Ficciones*
Weeks 9, 10, and 11   Thomas Pynchon, *Gravity's Rainbow*
Week 12   John Barth, *Lost in the Funhouse*
Week 13   Robert Coover, *The Universal Baseball Association*
Week 14   Modified hilarity and discussion of term papers.

(I chose to begin with *Herzog* precisely because it is not a radically experimental work, at least not in the terms that this class was considering, and for this reason could serve as a sort of sourcebook for narrative conventions that as readers most of us are inclined to accept as "ordinary" or "normal.") I generally ask classes during the first meeting whether anyone has read any of the assigned works before, and if so, in what context. I was interested to discover that only two out of twenty-two graduate students had read *The Golden Notebook* and that both of them had encountered the book in an undergraduate women's studies course.

After the first two weeks, classes were structured around student presentations, which generally lasted for ten to fifteen minutes and tried to set out the most pressing issues and questions arising from the work under discussion. Presenters familiarized themselves with the range of criticism on their books, although they were not required to deal explicitly with this criticism in class. As the seminar was a large one, there were usually two presenters, one beginning each hour of the two-hour session. Each presenter was assigned two respondents, who were to ask questions or comment on what seemed especially important in the presentation. The presenters met with me the day before the class to talk about the approaches they were planning to take, and on the basis of these discussions I prepared handouts of supporting material and my own class notes.

The feature that emerged as the most important constant in our reading of the first three postmodern novels was something that we ended up calling by the unwieldy name of ontological instability. In *Herzog*, as we observed (albeit mostly in retrospect—we tend to recognize conventions only after they have been called into question), we could clearly presume a stable fictional "reality," a state of affairs that remained constant regardless of how ignorant or self-deluded Herzog was, regardless of how much information about this state of affairs was made accessible to the reader. Indeed, judgments of ignorance or self-delusion, speculations about what we can or cannot know as readers, take for granted an underlying "real story" whose full or partial emergence may constitute much of the interest of the narrative structure. The books that we read after *Herzog* might seduce us with intimations of such a "real story," but to an overwhelming extent the staple plot question of realism and even of modernism—"What's really happening here?"— imported dubious premises into the reading of these books. We began to see that this question simply did not work, inasmuch as it led us into dead ends or into tricky either/or dilemmas in which the options were both mutually exclusive and flagrantly reductive.

For example, in Hawkes's *Second Skin*, the narrator-protagonist, Skipper, bears a superficial resemblance to Bellow's Moses Herzog, but he can be accused of romanticizing or fantasizing the events of his past only if we have some textual intimation of what "reality" might look like shorn of its romanticism and fantasy. Because Skipper recounts his adventures from the vantage of a paradisial "floating island" that has marked affinities with *The Tempest* and few affinities with documented natural phenomena, interpretations aimed at discerning the truth underlying Skipper's lyrical discourse end up constructing what becomes in effect another story: for instance, Skipper is "really" in a mental hospital and just *thinks* he is on a floating island. Such readings end up telling us more about what we habitually expect of stories than about what Hawkes gives us in this particular instance. In the same way, Margaret Atwood's *Lady Oracle* plays on the impossibility of distinguishing among real, invented, and hallucinated events and links this absence of familiar narrative and ontological boundaries to the impossibility of locating a "true" self that would reduce competing identities to the status of masquerades or misapprehensions. And Vladimir Nabokov's *Pale Fire* presents two texts, each a gloss on the other, each claiming the truth of autobiography and representing the other as a distortion.

Having negotiated the disconcerting loops on which these novels sent us, we arrived at the two weeks set aside for *The Golden Notebook* in an alert and rather suspicious frame of mind. I had divided the novel into two very unequal parts for the purposes of presentation and discussion: for the first class, the first three "Free Women" sections and their attendant notebooks (3–504); for the second class, the rest of the book (a mere 159 pages). I requested that the students *not* read Lessing's 1971 introduction, on the grounds that it both gave away the big structural surprise and simplified the implications of this surprise in ways that might prove misleading. (This was a tactical error: of course everybody read the introduction immediately. I had forgotten how graduate students lust after forbidden criticism.) I also suggested that there were ways in which the experience of reading *The Golden Notebook* might be significantly different from the experience of reading any of the preceding novels and that everyone might think about ways to pinpoint and articulate this difference.

The presenters were very aware of the difference when they met in my office to discuss their routes into Lessing's work. Whereas previous presentations had been based on close readings that exposed and discussed narrative strategies, both the young man and the young woman who were scheduled to open the discussion found that with *The Golden Notebook* they needed first of all to establish a context for the encyclopedic range of the five hundred pages they had just assimilated. The young man, who had agreed to begin the first hour, had ended up buttonholing a professor of twentieth-century history and eliciting a terrifying reading list dealing with the development and dispersal of the Communist party in the West. "It's kind of embarrassing I don't know this stuff," he admitted. "I think of myself as a Marxist." As we talked about the development of the Marxist line during the first half of the century and about the ideological affinities between Marxism and nineteenth-century realism, I started pulling out books and shuffling through them for key passages—Lessing's own reference to the nineteenth-century realist tradition as "the highest point of literature" in her essay "The Small Personal Voice"; Georg Lukács's prescriptions for successful narratives in "Narrate or Describe?" (127–29); and David Lodge's attempts to establish formal distinctions between realism and the ensuing texts of modernism and postmodernism (25, 47). We decided to transcribe about two pages of selections from these works for distribution to the class the next day.

The young woman was interested in the larger implications of this approach. "We're talking about the 'real world' here," she observed (like many of the members of the seminar, she habitually inscribed the quotation marks in the air with her fingertips). "It's a little like what we did with *Herzog*, but even more intense, as if there's a kind of realism that makes us fill in the background of historical reality. But at the same time, we've got this theme of the artist trying to create, and that's a modernist theme, especially when it's art in relation to chaotic reality. What's interesting is that this theme is working *with* the politics, especially the feminism, to make the realism unhappy. There's all this writing about how this writing isn't working. Something's going to happen to the shape of the novel." I applauded her. "It's something like *écriture féminine*," she ventured. "Not *like* it exactly, but the same kind of motivation."

The seminar exposed one of the key issues at stake in these comments. "I don't think you can call this book postmodern," one student observed. "I mean, even if the structure gets weirder, this isn't just messing around with conventions. This is serious." Discussion exploded over whether messing around with conventions isn't, in fact, serious, over what "serious" means in this and other literary contexts, and over whether experiments with narrative structure and style might occur because of explicitly political commitment rather than because of a wish to avoid or deny political concerns. By the end of the period, a great deal seemed to be hanging on our reading of the rest of the novel.

The two young women who were to be presenters for the second session arrived in my office in a state of high excitement. "I'm going to have to propose a change in terminology," said the first one. "We need to discriminate between Anna 1 and Anna 2. There are two separate lines of narration here, and they interconnect but you can't say either one is 'fictional' in relation to the other." "It's the dissolution of the subject," said the second one. "I want to mention Deleuze and Guattari's *Anti-Oedipus*. And of course Foucault." "And of course R. D. Laing," I said, and was gratified when they chorused "Who?" There are occasions, I am discovering, when the process of aging qualifies me as a historian.

These presentations involved more close reading than the previous ones, and they led us to the first really synthetic gesture of the seminar. Using *The Golden Notebook* as a paradigm, the students generated a list of thematic headings that I put on the blackboard: Writing, "Naming," and Literary Conventions; (Dis)Integration; The "Sex War" and Writing Other-Wise; and Explanatory Structures (this last encompassed both political Marxism and traditional psychoanalysis, along with some of the critical theories that individual members of the class had brought to bear on the novel). We then extended these categories to the other books we had read so far, and we tried to generalize about similarities and differences. One immediate outcome, already implicit in our discussions of innovation and seriousness, was that we finally began to get at the feminism of *Lady Oracle* and in this way to approach the question of gender as a determinant of structural and stylistic experimentation. A more comprehensive outcome was that we went on to the other works on the syllabus with a much more developed understanding of how self-reflexivity in fiction might not necessarily entail self-absorption or aestheticism.

Much of the success of this approach to *The Golden Notebook* was due to the intelligence, preparation, and motivation of the individual graduate students who constituted the seminar. I plan to repeat the format this year, but of course I have no assurance of comparable results. I can, however, reflect on some of the ways in which the syllabus and class structure helped produce what still strikes me as an extraordinarily insightful and provocative treatment of Lessing's novel (and, not incidentally, helped produce several excellent term papers).

First of all, this class entered *The Golden Notebook* by the back door, so to speak. The novel *is* history because of the way it was embraced by a whole generation, but this generation (emphatically my own) embraced it because of its subject matter. The passionate readings of those of us who looked at the two women alone in a London flat and saw our own reflections established *The Golden Notebook* as a classic, but our claims on the book also led subsequent readers to approach it as a document defining an era and a set of problems and kept us all away from the "wordless statement" that Lessing insisted was inherent in the structure. My class looked for structural anomalies, found meanings, and settled down to consider the ways in which structure might mean.

Second, the environment of other metafictions ("I see you're teaching Tricky Books again," remarked one of my more caustic colleagues) allowed the class to recognize the playful and parodic aspects of *The Golden Notebook* without feeling as if they were violating some overall tone of high seriousness and to view Lessing's abrupt changes in style and emphasis as bravura performances rather than as embarrassing lapses. On the other hand, Lessing's differences also acquired dignity from the contrast, and members of the seminar frequently referred back to the "seriousness" of her political themes as we discussed later books on the syllabus.

Third—and this may be the most important single observation—Lessing acquired status by virtue of being associated with members of an acknowledged male avant-garde. I have all sorts of mixed feelings about this situation, but it is undoubtedly real, and it came home to me with special poignancy when one of the young women in the class, a feminist activist and incipient feminist critic, bounced into my office to report on her enthusiasm for the book. "I'd heard about it, of course," she said. "But I didn't know it was interesting *too*." "Interesting" is perhaps the highest praise that a graduate student in my department can bestow on a literary work. Given the context, I could only agree that *The Golden Notebook* is indeed interesting. Too.

The Golden Notebook and Creative Writing Majors

Ruth Saxton

Mills College, where I teach, is an independent liberal arts college for women. Many English majors at Mills are creative writing students or MFA candidates who, arriving at Mills with a resistance to literary-critical analysis, pose particular challenges for professors of English literature. They do not want to analyze literature; they want to create it. While I feel no obligation to give students only what they want, I do consider their preferences and the gaps in their knowledge and skills when I plan a class. Over the last twelve years I have noticed that the "Pentimento" modeling assignment I give in my freshman English courses is often a favorite assignment of creative writing students. I have recently begun to include such assignments in my literature courses as a way to introduce students to analysis.

Students in my advanced courses are already familiar with my "Pentimento" assignment: "Write a four-to-six-page paper modeled after one of the chapters in Lillian Hellman's *Pentimento*, revealing your own change and growth by focusing on a significant person you have known for some time." To write this paper, students have to read and analyze Hellman's book, a work of autobiographical fiction, each chapter of which describes a person of major importance in her life. They gain assurance as they locate the subtle as well as the obvious structures of Hellman's text, and they enjoy borrowing her opening devices—beginning their papers with a letter or other document (as in "Bethe") or with a startling assertion (as in "Willy"). Students appreciate being asked to do something new, something outside their accustomed writing mode. One indication of the way this assignment engages students and gives them a format they do not assume they have down pat (like the dread five-paragraph essay) is that in the twelve years I have required such papers, no student has ever neglected to pick up her graded paper from my office.

Students tell me that by borrowing the structures of Hellman's chapters, they have been able to give shape to their own most frightening experiences and insights. They say they cannot write about the alcoholic father, the mother's psychotic breakdown, the sadistic lover, the attempted suicide in expository essays with theses and still tell the truth. The pain blurs too much. Somehow in forcing their material into a particular and fictionalized form, they become writers with the power to shape the telling of their truths—even in a freshman English class.

When I began developing an advanced seminar on Doris Lessing and realized that over half of the students enrolled in the course were either MFA candidates or seniors with an emphasis in creative writing, I decided to include an imitation assignment similar to the "Pentimento" paper. I reasoned that such an assignment would especially help the creative writing students improve their repertoires of writing strategies, would enable them to appreciate the skill of professional writers, and would indirectly introduce them to analysis.

On the first day of the Lessing seminar, I announced that students would have a choice of final projects: either a fifteen-to-twenty-page critical essay or a "Golden Notebook" paper of the same length. I described the latter option as follows:

> Read *The Golden Notebook*, and write your own "Golden Notebook" in which you interweave a conventional work of fiction with a series of notebooks. After careful analysis of Lessing's handling of material in the notebooks, choose three or four colors to represent disparate parts of your protagonist's life. The entire assignment should be from fifteen to twenty typed, double-spaced pages, including a one-to-three-page explanation that, like Lessing's preface to the 1972 edition, explains what you are trying to do.

This approach helps students gain some distance from a literary work and from their own lives, a distance often necessary for them to begin writing in response to a text. Lessing's works are demanding. They disturb and probe our psyches until no crevice is left unexposed, thus evoking our emotions as well as our thoughts on everything from the most public and political to the most private topics. Our engagement is part of what brings us repeatedly back to her work; it also can make writing about her texts draining and intimidating. My students ranged in age from twenty to sixty; some of them had read all of Lessing before coming to college and were eager to discuss her work, while others had to ask who she was and took the class for the usual reasons—the time, the teacher, a friend's recommendation.

Students who read her for the first time were as struck by Lessing's insights as I had been fifteen years ago. They identified with one character after another. I could understand that initial sense of recognition and identification. Sometimes as a middle-aged woman I feel almost as if I am becoming a character in a Lessing novel—haunted by the projectionist, constantly observing, defining, judging the emotions, the relationships, the self with a relentless, questing mind. Indeed, I often have to set her work aside, seeking a respite, as she forces me to face things I would rather avoid. I wondered if my students would also need that respite, especially from *The Golden Notebook*. The "Pentimento" model, I felt, could offer them a distance from Lessing's texts similar to the distance they have in reading, for instance, a nineteenth-century novel.

To write a "Golden Notebook" paper, students had to be intimately acquainted with *The Golden Notebook*. I gave the following preliminary assignments for students to consider before reading the novel:

1. If you keep a diary or journal, skim your entries for the past six months and list categories by which you might classify them—for example, school or work, role as mother or daughter, friendship, politics, religion, love or sex. If you do not keep a journal, list possible categories about which you often think and might be able to write if you were to keep a journal. What three or four areas are major preoccupations?
2. What do you expect of fiction? What is the responsibility of the novelist? Write an exploratory journal entry in which you respond to these questions.
3. Is it possible to tell the truth in fiction? Write a paragraph in which you answer yes and a second paragraph in which you answer no. Explain both answers.
4. In-class assignment: Write for five minutes about an important incident in your life this past week, writing in first person as you would in your journal or in a letter to a friend. Now, write that same incident in third person, treating yourself as a character and giving her a fictitious name.
5. Choose a day on which to be conscious of all that you do. Either that evening or the next day, write the most complete memoir possible of what you did, thought, felt.

All students in the class carried out the five exercises whether or not they eventually chose to write a "Golden Notebook" paper. The exercises led into our discussion of the novel and provided a balance in the work of the course. Lessing, Anna, and Ella blur in a reading of *The Golden Notebook*, and readers tend to equate Anna Wulf and Doris Lessing just as they often equate Jane Eyre and Charlotte Brontë. When fictional and autobiographical content share so much, it is difficult to draw definitive lines between fact and fiction. The discussions of telling the truth, fictionalizing autobiography, and defining the novelist's responsibility were animated as students wrestled with their sense of responsibility and of truth telling in the writing of their exercises and papers.

Reading *The Golden Notebook*, students recognized connections between the early assignments and Lessing's text. They enjoyed choosing colors for each of their notebooks and began to notice the subtle connections between notebook material and the content of "Free Women." Those working on the project found it much easier to fragment their journal entries into several notebooks than to work between their own conventional fiction and their notebooks. It was difficult to fictionalize notebook material, and for many students the notebook entries were actual accounts of their experiences, concerns, doubts. For others, the notebook entries were attributed to fictional protagonists.

Several literature majors as well as creative writing students chose the modeling assignment as an alternative to the usual critical paper. It helped them, paradoxically, to develop the analytical skills they needed for writing more conventional critical essays. The initial work of analyzing the text may even have been more rigorous than that required for a critical essay. Though students did not have to focus a critical argument and formulate a thesis, they had to study the text with great care.

Students writing the "Golden Notebook" paper became my most outspoken and precise students in discussion. They supported their opinions with reference to specific instances in the text. In trying to discover a model for their papers, they noticed features of Lessing's novel missed by less careful readers. For example, as they struggled with how to apportion their own notebook material, they noticed the page-length variations in Anna's notebooks. They registered the effect of Anna's making one notebook, the black one, the longest and of her beginning with that notebook. They debated the effect of including news clippings, capsule short story plots, dreams. As they moved between Lessing's text and their own, they developed strongly felt opinions about her novel, opinions that enriched seminar discussions and led to assertions that formed the basis of later critical essays. Their writing also helped them appreciate the importance of the "Golden Notebook" chapter of Lessing's novel, since many of them were unable to write a comparable chapter. They discovered that although their papers had borrowed the surface structure of the Lessing novel, they had not shared Lessing's underlying preoccupation with fragmentation, breakdown, and unity.

What were the logistics of the assignment beyond the preliminary exercises? We devoted two weeks of class discussion to *The Golden Notebook* midway through the semester, and I encouraged students to finish the book before we began that discussion. (I had devoted the first week of the semester to lecture material about Lessing while students began reading a selection of her short stories for discussion the second week. By midsemester, they were accustomed to discussing a previously read text while reading the next one.) We focused discussion for our four seminar meetings on *The Golden Notebook* as follows.

Session 1: "Free Women," part 1, and the notebooks that immediately follow

Session 2: "Free Women," parts 2 and 3, and the notebooks that follow each

Session 3: "Free Women," parts 4 and 5, the remaining notebooks, and the "Golden Notebook"

Session 4: the preface to the 1972 edition and any three published critical articles on *The Golden Notebook*, including one written before 1972

Students who hated to write critical papers were able to shed much of their fear of analysis. Their analyses of the novels we read after *The Golden Notebook* were more thorough than their earlier ones, at least in part because analysis had been demystified. And, as might be expected, some of those students who had formerly avoided "creative writing" discovered delight in writing an imaginative paper for the first time. An indirect approach to criticism by way of imitation helps erode the false dichotomy between creative writing and literary criticism, between writing and reading, and between writer and reader.

PEDAGOGICAL CHALLENGES AND OPPORTUNITIES

The Golden Notebook and Undergraduates: Strategies for Involving Students

Sharon Hileman

The Golden Notebook can of course be approached as a realistic novel concerned with issues and dilemmas of the modern world. But in addition to discussing such features when teaching the novel, I like to have students spend some time investigating the work as a self-conscious novel that deliberately calls attention to its fictional status. This approach helps them see that there really is a difference between Anna Wulf and Doris Lessing, a distinction easily blurred when a writer writes about a writer. I emphasize Lessing's overt attempts to show us how fiction is made and how fiction remains fiction.

As part of the background to the novel, I present some of Lessing's comments indicating the problematic relation between matter and manner in this work. These include statements from the original novel's dust jacket: "I understood that the shape of the book should be so enclosed and claustrophobic—so narcissistic that the subject matter must break through the form," as well as remarks from an interview quoted in *A Small Personal Voice*: "it was a highly structured book, carefully planned. The point of that book was the relation of its parts to each other" (51).

Students have several specific assignments as we work through the novel, beginning with keeping time lines and outlines for each notebook's first installment. I ask them to list dates and then briefly mention the important characters and events described in each notebook. This assignment, which corresponds with the first reading assignment, allows first-time readers to sort out the numerous events, characters, and narrative redundancies within the text and retain a written record of them.

During class, students form four groups to compare and discuss their outlines for these first installments of the four notebooks. I ask each group to make a brief presentation to the rest of the class summarizing their decisions about the major occurrences detailed in each notebook and speculating about the purpose of each specific notebook. (I prefer to have students use these inductive methods to determine the different notebooks' functions rather than provide them with this material as part of the introduction to the novel.) In one class, the different groups wrote their time lines on the board, revealing a major discrepancy between the black and blue notebooks.

Anna's first entry in the diary, dated 7 January 1950, alludes to Max Wulf, whom she says she has written about as Willi in the black notebook. But the black notebook doesn't seem to begin until 1951, and there is no reference to Willi in it until 1954. Now the class must try to determine whether Lessing is guilty of an oversight or whether she is deliberately showing us Anna's need to fictionalize, which Anna herself has denounced in the diary's opening remarks.

I point out that the novel is often interpreted as a progression from fiction to fact, with facts ultimately providing a vision of "truth." Thus the novel begins with "Free Women," a fictionalized version of the experience that follows it in the notebooks. Moving through the notebooks, according to this reading, strips away the past (memory's fiction), the political (vested interest's fiction), and the avowedly fictional (the self's fiction). Then Anna is left with the blue notebook, the diary, in which to escape from fiction and find herself. But if the blue notebook is still fiction, there may be nothing to accept as "real" in the novel.

The question of what is "real" in fiction cannot be resolved at this point (or perhaps at any other point), so I now introduce some background material on the self-conscious novel, using characteristics described by Robert Alter in *Partial Magic: The Novel as a Self-Conscious Genre*. Alter's definition of the self-conscious novel as an artwork mirroring itself as it mirrors nature and thus tending to reproduce itself *en abîme* with Chinese-box constructions seems particularly applicable to *The Golden Notebook*. This is especially true of the yellow notebook, which most clearly embodies a fiction within a fiction within a fiction. By this time the class has read the fourth "Free Women" and notebook installments, so I now have them do additional group work related to the yellow notebook. Again I ask for time lines and outlines, now for the second, third, and fourth installments of the yellow notebook.

I ask the fourth group to develop a list of the correlations they see between the last yellow and blue notebook installments (since both contain the nineteen numbered references). As we prepare to discuss our findings, I review the summary we have already made of the first yellow notebook. These presentations lead us into a discussion of the making and interpreting of fiction as we consider Anna's "realistic" portrayal of Ella, Anna's self-critique of her attempts to create the fictional Ella, Anna's identification and non-identification with Ella, Anna/Ella's lists of possible stories, and then the end of the yellow notebook (which is, however, continued in the final blue notebook's numbered entries).

The last idea for a story in the yellow notebook is "The Romantic Tough School of Writing" (539), such an obvious parody that it compels Anna to terminate the notebook. Defining parody as the device that calls attention to language as an artificial structure that can be manipulated, we then look for other examples of it in this yellow notebook.

I provide some commentary on parody as another device of self-conscious fiction and then have the class find some of the numerous examples of parody in the other notebooks. In the second segment of the black notebook, for instance, when all readers have become aware of the symbolic function of the different colors of the notebooks, there is obvious parody in the use of colors. Written correspondence between Anna and a television agent includes invitations for a drink at the Black Bull, lunch at the Red Baron, another lunch at the White Tower. Several pages later Anna describes a letter from a different agent who represents the Bluebird Series and invites her to Black's Hotel for a drink.

Should we interpret this as Anna's own parodying of her use of the different notebooks? Or is this an example of Lessing parodying her entire novel? The question is impossible to answer. But by asking and trying to answer these kinds of questions, students confront some of the problems with language that characterize this text. And again I am reminding them that authors and narrators are separate entities.

We now come to the chapter entitled "The Golden Notebook," which shows that answers to questions in fiction may simply raise more questions. After some six hundred pages, most readers must radically alter their readings of the novel when they discover that Anna Wulf, not an omniscient narrator or authorial voice, is author and narrator of "Free Women." Are we to believe, next, that Anna's consciousness is supposed to have shaped the entire novel *The Golden Notebook*?

This question of the narrator's identity is the final one that students consider as they now look back through the work as a whole. Who has written the bracketed passages? If Anna is the narrator, why has she referred to herself in the third rather than first person in many of those passages? And why were some of these passages considered necessary? Do we really need to be told, "A date was scribbled here," right before 1951 appears in the notebook? As we discuss these questions, we probe further into the relation between reality and real-seeming artifice.

Now we are ready to pool the lists we have been making since the inception of our reading. I ask students to keep a list of all the writers and different kinds of writing that are used or referred to in the notebooks, including mentions of the pieces of writing ostensibly taped, gummed, or stapled into the notebooks. Here we see to what extent Lessing has bombarded us with forms of writing and evidence of its fictionality. To read *The Golden Notebook* is to encounter—within a novella and five notebooks—references to other works of fiction, including *Frontiers of War*, "The Shadow of the Third," and Saul Green's novel about the Algerian soldier; nineteen numbered ideas for stories and novels; letters; an old diary, old papers, old lists; book reviews; the magazine *Women at Home*; television brochures; Saul Green's love letters and diaries; Communist propaganda; allusions to Mann, Austen, Stendhal, Proust, Tolstoy, Thomas Wolfe, Gissing, George Eliot; material such as newspaper clippings, "scribbled sheets," "lined writing paper," and carbons of other people's stories that have been pasted or pinned into the notebooks. (And this is only a partial list.) The novel becomes claustrophobic, as Lessing herself specified it should be, but in the sense that it allows no escape from the world of writing, especially the desire to fictionalize, which stands behind so much of the written word. Clearly Lessing has given us not just a realistic novel. Structurally *The Golden Notebook* may seem to move from most fictionalized to least fictionalized experience, but again and again, through its incorporation of innumerable forms of writing, the novel demonstrates its own fictionality.

We conclude that *The Golden Notebook* is not just a realistic novel about a woman writer. It is a book about writing that approaches its subject from a number of different perspectives. Since the subject we are discussing is writing and since most students taking this class have just completed freshman composition courses, I like to have them experiment with some of Lessing's techniques. I believe we teachers usually do not have students do enough writing in literature classes and that a work like *The Golden Notebook* makes it very easy to integrate personal writing into a noncomposition course. (These assignments can be given as short exercises that correspond with lecture or discussion sessions or they can be used after discussing the entire novel.)

The first problem Anna confronts as she looks back at the black notebook is its dishonesty, emanating from nostalgia. As an exercise in investigating this problem, I ask students to write short papers (300–500 words) about a past event in their lives that is associated with a particular place, group of people, or significant personal relationship. After students write the papers, I have them form small groups and read several of their peers' essays, trying to determine whether the writing is nostalgic. Once they've read about four essays (written by people who are not in their group), we have a general discussion. I ask what Anna meant in labeling her Mashopi material nostalgic, whether or not students see nostalgia in one another's writing, and what the criteria are for labeling certain writing nostalgic in the first place.

Another way to get at the problem of truthful writing that concerns Anna is to consider, as she does, the question of audience. I ask students how what they write for themselves is different from what they write for others, and we discuss the difference between chaos and order that Anna mentions in considering this issue. Then students write a short account of a major emotional experience they've had (involving love, fear, anger, shock, and so on) for themselves only. Next I ask them to turn that material into a fictionalized account (that I read). Excellent creative writing often results from this assignment, and having done it, students are ready to talk about Anna's comments concerning the creation of characters. The question of where the dividing line between creator and created appears is another way of turning the discussion to Lessing and reminding students that Anna is in fact a character in a novel herself.

One more writing exercise that eventually makes students confront the problem of truth that plagues Anna is similar to her experiment in one of the blue notebooks. Anna was trying to avoid the untruthful shaping or patterning of experience that occurs in writing about a series of events. She tried to list events objectively and chronologically but was dissatisfied with that attempt. Then she condensed the material into a one-paragraph summary, trying to compensate for having been too aware of occurrences and perhaps detailing them too fully. Another time she decided it was impossible to achieve what she wanted by writing; only a film could convey the nuances she desired.

I have students deal with a variation of the problem (and show me they are keeping up with reading assignments) by giving them about ten minutes at the end of several classes to write in response to specific questions. As soon as they've read about one-third of the novel, I ask them to free write about everything they think is interesting, important, problematic about Anna. After they've read about two-thirds of the work, I ask the same basic question but now elicit any new insights or changed opinions they may have developed. Finally, when they've completed the entire novel, I ask them to write a summarizing character sketch of Anna. These reading quizzes show remarkably diverse spectrums of response. Often the difficulty students experience in beginning the novel is expressed in their dislike of Anna or their lack of sympathy for her. Usually the negative character sketches they write as early reactions to the novel are radically different from their final sketches. This transformation reminds me that reading, like writing, is a process, and that changes in perspective affect response. I can share this insight with students by returning their quizzes on the last day of our discussion and asking them to decide which is the most "truthful" of their responses.

These writing assignments can be quickly and easily done. They emanate from personal experience and can be used to begin discussions of major questions raised by the novel. Most important, giving the class opportunities to read one another's writings allows them to establish greater rapport with one another, resulting in more animated general discussions.

Since so much of *The Golden Notebook* is concerned with questions and problems of writing, it is easy to justify having students write in response to their reading experiences. When they themselves grapple with the very things that are being described in a work, students who are not political, not feminists, not aspiring novelists can still find some sort of relevance in *The Golden Notebook*. A few have even decided it is the best book they've ever read.

Illusions of Actuality:
First-Person Pronoun in *The Golden Notebook*

Virginia Tiger

> I got angry over reviews of *The Golden Notebook*. They
> thought it very personal—it was in parts. . . . the book
> they tried to turn it into was: The Confessions of Doris
> Lessing.
>
> Doris Lessing, *Small Personal Voice*

"It struck me that my . . . turning everything into fiction . . . must be an evasion. . . . Why do I never write down, simply, what happens," Anna Wulf's first blue-notebook entry records (229), giving testimony to the self-reflexive narrator and self-referential text at the center of *The Golden Notebook*'s concerns. For—despite the "Free Women" aerobic exercise in third-person fictive production—*The Golden Notebook* is substantively a fiction narrated in the first person by a self-reflexive autobiographical persona, herself an author-heroine obsessed with the problematics of narrative mimesis, veracity, and self-referentiality. "I decided to use the blue notebook . . . as nothing but a record of facts. Every evening I sat . . . and wrote down my day, and it was as if I, Anna, were nailing Anna to the page. Every day I shaped Anna" (476), an almost vertiginous narrator observes later, dissecting the displacement of "I" into "Anna," fact into artifact. Among other matters, the fictionalized "I" here is introducing the indeterminate relation of autobiography and fiction. Yet who is this "I" who utters?

So I query graduate students as they ponder the transformations of lives into literatures; our seminar, one on autobiographical encodings, includes such canonical texts as Jean-Jacques Rousseau's *Confessions*, Virginia Woolf's *To the Lighthouse*, D. H. Lawrence's *Sons and Lovers*, Gertrude Stein's *Autobiography of Alice B. Toklas*, James Joyce's *Portrait of the Artist as a Young Man*, George Eliot's *Mill on the Floss*, and selections from Anaïs Nin's *Diaries*. Perhaps more than any of these other fictions, *The Golden Notebook* offers a sunken shipload of critical treasures, for from its pages concerns that have dominated work in narrative theory for the last decade can be retrieved and their taxonomies detailed. Fictional self-reference, a narrative's announcement of its own fictiveness, is amply evident in the book's fractured structure as well as systematically flaunted in the collusions of colliding plot duplications and character doubles. For students to read *The Golden Notebook* in this context, then, is for them to confront mercurial conundrums about autobiography, confession, biography, fictional autobiography, and autobiographical fiction as well as the fictiveness of the writing enterprise itself.

Practicing here what we now call a deconstructive form of writing, Doris Lessing questions (in a tone unfashionably earnest) the duplicities inherent in discourse. Her distrust of narrative authority is signaled by a text gelatinous with fractured fictions: interleaved notebooks, journal notations, plots and story outlines, film scenarios and novelistic anecdotes, a conventional novel frame to whose thin skeleton adhere diary entries, reviews, pastiches, parodies. Like Anna Wulf marooned by newspaper clippings pinned round her walls, Doris Lessing seems islanded by a forest of broken texts. And by restless impersonations voicing a narrative I.

In-class reports by students focus on matters like these and on the kaleidoscopic reflections of Anna as the reader twists from the middle distance of "Free Women" 1 through the regressive editorial commentary ("[The four notebooks were identical . . . as if Anna had, almost automatically, divided herself into four . . .]") to the foregrounded first sentences of black notebook 1: "Every time I sit down to write, and let my mind go easy . . ." (55, 56). Inevitably students conclude that the controlling author is present, preventing the reader from settling comfortably into the illusion of a closed fictional world. Yet invariably they are disquieted by Lessing's violation of mimetic integrity. Specifically, two self-referential narrative devices in the text make the students frown with impatience. The first is the infringement on the novel's closure caused by the two very different conclusions for Anna's "life." It becomes somewhat less baffling if we turn to extratextual considerations such as Rachel DuPlessis's observation that women writers need to disrupt conventional narrative endings—to practice "writing beyond the ending" (103). For their close analyses of *The Golden Notebook*'s structure, exegeses by such Lessing scholars as John L. Carey, Martha Lifson, and Claire Sprague (*Rereading*) are also informative in this context.

Far more startling a break with readerly expectations of a hermetically sealed fictional universe is the second self-referential strategy: the source for *The Golden Notebook*'s limpidly simple first sentence: "The two women were alone in the London flat." Discovering—all but at *The Golden Notebook*'s end—that "Free Women" is not "about" the Anna who writes the notebooks but is a fictively autobiographical projection of the Anna of the notebooks catapults students into branches high enough for them to chatter like worried starlings. Their dislocation arises, of course, because they have read "Free Women" from the perspective of the very convention *The Golden Notebook* is violating. Paradoxically, however, "Free Women" proposes that its reader apprehend its characters and incidents as fictional entities when indeed they are mirrored fictive constructs: fictional Anna of the notebooks has invented fictive Anna of "Free Women" just as certainly as she invented fictive Ella of "The Shadow of the Third."

Students by and large expect fictional characters to achieve an integrated identity, all the more if the students have been exploring autobiographical fictions that, like Joyce's *Portrait* and Lawrence's *Sons and Lovers,* map what has been called the "artist-hero's odyssey to self-knowledge" (Foley 188). A correlative expectation that the text should be autotelic rises from the same (unexamined) belief in mimesis, realism, and—possibly—liberal humanism. However much one explains—pointing to Roland Barthes, Vladimir Nabokov, Max Frisch—that postmodernists herald their own fictiveness, that narrators as characters within fictional worlds authoring fictive documents (that themselves constitute part of the narrative text) are common figures even in such popular novels as Bernard Malamud's *Dubin's Lives,* William Styron's *Sophie's Choice,* or Philip Roth's *Ghost Writer,* that one is supposed to have one's expectations bruised, a disconsolate student is sure to mutter that Lessing as author is untrustworthy. Once the reader's working premise about the implied author has been breached, the reader concludes that the authorizing agent is unreliable, the text an exercise in sleight of hand. Fictive Anna—namely, "Free Women" Anna—such students declare, has become more "fictional" (that is, less ontologically "real") than fictional Anna—namely, notebook Anna—whose "existence" now seems so saturated with "reality."

At this moment precisely, the instructor should write on opposite sides of a blackboard the following two sentences:

> I have only to write a phrase like "I walked down the street," or take a phrase from a newspaper "economic measures which lead to the full use of . . ." and immediately the words dissolve, and my mind starts spawning images which have nothing to do with the words, so that every word I see or hear seems like a small raft bobbing about on an enormous sea of images.   (476; blue notebook 3)

> That evening, sitting on the floor, playing jazz, desperate because of her inability to "make sense" out of the bits of [news]print, she felt a new sensation, like a hallucination, a new and hitherto not understood picture of the world.   (652; "Free Women" 5)

And then ask how the two materials, with shared thematic commonalities, differ. Is there a transformation from the (fictional) notebook to the (fictive) autobiographical novel? Does the second discourse seem muted in comparison with the first? Is this connected to a system of tenses? the distancing of the subject? In the discussion that follows, one student will dissect, unaware possibly of the term for this exercise, the privileging of the pronouns employed.

The instructor can now suggest that the choice of the pronoun *I* or *she* proposes a contract for the reader, a "reading contract" that—according to

Philippe Lejeune's provocative diagnoses (27–47)—shapes both a text's read-ing and its writing. Intimidated as they have already been by the duplica-tions, mirrorings, replayings, and parodic subversions that constitute *The Golden Notebook*'s self-referential text, students will now settle back, guarded by wry, none-too-diffident grins. For we approach the interrelated if second narratological issue the novel witnesses: the problematics of the autobio-graphical enterprise.

The characteristic readerly response of the class to confessional literature, an audience-speaker identification, has become more sophisticated at this stage in our analyses of the course's texts. No longer is the writer seen as merely mirrored biographically in his or her work. First readings, so re-ductively biographical and mimetic as to posit that Mrs. Morel *is* Mrs. Lawrence as surely as Mr. Ramsay *is* Mr. Stephen, have given way to an understanding that fictive impersonations occur when writers—claiming to tell truths by duplication (Rousseau here the sublime example)—write of their retrospective selves from a vantage point in the present. Admitting to the lure of autobiography, its gossip succulence, the private pleasures of figuring out biographical sources for stories, and the mass-media exploitation of the genre, students insist on its obligation to tell, more or less, a life story grounded in verifiable fact. What they will not accept is the modernist bias—one Doris Lessing shares—that autobiography and the confessional mode are imaginatively inferior to works of fiction.

On this subject, Lessing is famously cranky, dismissing biographical par-allels in works as obviously autobiographical as the Martha Quest series while admonishing critics for not attending to encodings in *The Memoirs of a Survivor*, which she describes as "an attempt at an autobiography." Since her definition only eccentrically refers to a work's veracity—what Elizabeth Bruss terms the "verification, truth-value" (7) distinguishing autobiography from fiction—distinctions such as Lessing erects between fact and fiction are tenuous.

Viable boundary lines, of course, can be drawn between historiography, biography, and autobiography, but not so easily between autobiography and fiction (Stelzig 21, 23). Indeed, some would argue that "[a]utobiography is fiction and fiction is autobiography. Both are narrative arrangements of real-ity" (Elbaz 187). Having shifted from generic classifications to deconstructive notions of textual productivity (the "endless" process of the text's produc-tivity), recent critical theory has stressed the affective bond between reader, writer, and text rather than autobiography's accountability to biography. Thus Roy Pascal's assertion in *Design and Truth in Autobiography* that autobiography, although a "coherent shaping of the past" (4), ranks as aes-thetically inferior to fiction and James Olney's declaration that there may be "no way to bring autobiography to heel as a literary genre with its own proper form, terminology, and observances" (3) have been supplanted by Paul de Man's explicitly Derridean observation that we confront in auto-biography not a life but a construction of a life (921). John Sturrock and Lejeune, the latter exploring the linguistic functioning of the first-person pronoun in autobiographical texts, endorse autobiographical narrative as fiction, situating the autobiographer's posture as autobiographer in the text. For "[h]ow can he [the writer] keep using the first-person pronoun, his sense of self-reference, without its becoming—since it becomes, in the course of writing, something other than strictly his own self-referential sign—a de facto third-person pronoun?" (Renza 9). From this perspective, autobio-graphical fiction (unlike autobiography) invokes a generic contract requiring the reader to see the text's characters as fictional replications, not biograph-ical duplications. Anna Wulf—fictional or fictive—is not Doris Lessing, the class decides.

It does, that is, until it hears one forehead-furrowed individual expostulate that the novelistic veil of *The Golden Notebook* is actually very thin. "Good lord! Take a look at that 'Golden Notebook' passage where Anna's having a dream about Saul Green and imagines he's a tiger." Here, Anna records, "I must write a play about Anna and Saul and the tiger" (616). Doris Lessing she may not be, but Anna Freeman Wulf plans nonetheless to write the very drama (about Anna Freeman and a rootless American) that under the title *Play with a Tiger* Doris Lessing wrote and had produced at the Royal Court Theatre, concurrently with the publication of *The Golden Notebook*. Unquestionably, the reference to an extratextual reality, a classic technique of autobiography, disrupts the fictional status of *The Golden Notebook*.

Emboldened so, students are quick then to assemble other material to argue their view that the internal "Golden Notebook" and the blue notebooks (in effect, first-person diaries) are encodings of autobiographical sources. "The blue notebooks may even *be* actual notebooks that Doris Lessing wrote earlier when she felt miserable," observes one class member. As "verifica-tion, truth-value" another student quotes Lessing's comments during an interview in France when several of her books appeared in French editions, some two decades after *The Golden Notebook*'s publication. With rare can-dor, Lessing here admitted to having been so devastated by a liaison with a man ("un homme très destructeur, un psychiatre") that she worked with a therapist ("avec une femme, une jungienne") during her thirties (interview, with Rihoit, 51).

Extratextually then, blue notebooks 1 and 2 with their record of Anna's hurt liaison with Michael, the psychiatrist, and the replay of her sessions with the Jungian, Mrs. Marks, carry more than the laundry list of confessional veracity. Extratextually again, Anna's duplication of herself as Anna and as Ella—"I, Anna, see Ella. Who is, of course, Anna" (459)—can be taken as evidence of Lessing's more than strategic use of her own life in her fiction. Citing from *Going Home* the 1957 statement "I have notebooks which are full of stories, plots, anecdotes, which at one time or another I was impelled to write" (164), the students finally insist that could one examine Lessing's early drafts for *The Golden Notebook*, one would find again "verification, truth-value" for the autobiographical status of the "I."

First-person narrative often collapses distinctions between author and narrator, conflating an author's grammatical subject with the subject who narrates the plot, I remark, citing the blue-notebook sentence written on the blackboard. Third-person narration, witness here the juxtaposed passage from "Free Women," erects a barrier between author and text, discouraging in turn an intimacy between author and reader. This may explain, I suggest, the students' sense that fictive Anna Wulf of "Free Women" is less onto-logically real than fictional Anna of the notebooks. Turning to those sections in the yellow notebooks where Lessing has her persona Anna self-consciously impersonate herself as Ella, I borrow Wayne Booth's insight in *The Rhetoric of Fiction*. As Booth instructs, when the fictional "I" becomes a self-sufficient persona, the metaphoric myopia of that "I" can be discredited without im-plicating the all-powerful author. First-person authorial personae endorse distancing devices, of course: defensive displacements that paradoxically permit an author's narrative inflation of self.

Deliberately left to the end here is a discussion of what readers now take as *The Golden Notebook*'s preface, an apologia cum advertisement that ap-peared first in a 1971 *Partisan Review* (nine years after the novel's publi-cation) and henceforth was affixed—as authorial introduction—to later editions of the text. Teaching the text, I (try to) enforce the recommendation that students first read the novel and then situate their submission to this authorial command. For like Henry James's poised, near petulant introductions and Bernard Shaw's lugubriously didactic prefaces, Lessing's piece amounts to a highly stylized autobiographical account of the genesis of her creation, what a deconstructionist would call a production. The term aside, having read the *Partisan* article, the reader is all but compelled to assent to its material about intentionality and thereby almost always must read *The Golden Notebook* in the light of that autobiographical persona's claims that the book was about fragmentation, division, "a wordless statement," and so on.

My view, rather different from the one presented in this "preface," is that fissured texts like *The Golden Notebook* and the repetitive assertion of bi-ography in all its first-person impersonations (two narrative strategies that inform other of Lessing's writings as well) evoke a chaos of absence, the preoedipal mother whose nonpresence must be punished by the assertion of self-identity, self-referentiality, self-reflexiveness. Psychologically moth-erless, such an author—as Janine Chasseguet-Smirgel might posit—converts primary ontological negation into brave acts of pious daring: the "I" who utters.

Do students accept such readings? If at all, only reluctantly, of course. The seminar closes with an agreement that position papers be individually developed; the two narratological matters—referentiality and autobiographicality—must be tested. And one text, the following, a passage from the inner "Golden Notebook," is used, beginning with a numerical count of the "I":

> The idea for this story intrigued me, and I began thinking how it should be written. How, for instance, would it change if I used Ella instead of myself? I had not thought about Ella for some time. . . . I began imagining how she would be with Saul—much more intelligent, I think, than I, cooler, for instance. After a while I realised I was doing what I had done before, creating "the third"—the woman altogether better than I was. . . . Then I began to laugh because of the distance between what I was imagining and what in fact I was, let alone what Ella was.   (637)

Like Van Gogh's portrait of his room at Arles, the bed and chair and vista redolent with the artist's presence by the artist's placement of his absence, Lessing's *Golden Notebook* here is as well a complex tapestry of intent and fictionality and "I" performance. It invites its inventor to enter—and the wary student to explore the puzzles of the autobiographical enterprise's illusions of actuality.

The Golden Notebook:
A Feminist Context for the Classroom

Mona Knapp

In both scholarly and popular essays of the last fifteen years, it has become almost commonplace to initiate any discussion of modern feminist literature by mentioning *The Golden Notebook*. No work of fiction had more impact on the women's movement of the 1960s and 1970s. A feminist critique of this novel in the classroom is, considering its reception as the very symbol of feminism, inevitable. A feminist approach to teaching it should not only seek to help students better understand the novel but, in doing so, use the text to enhance the reader's comprehension of social and political movements per se, far beyond the limits of the classroom.

But a feminist critique automatically triggers a series of questions far more unwieldy than the usual classroom fare. Not the least of these is the task of providing some basic historical and theoretical background, since feminist criticism—like Marxist criticism—cannot be used in oblivion to the ideas and events that produced it. Because many students see themselves as already liberated postfeminists who "don't need" feminism, the groundwork must be laid by defining, at least broadly, the climate that welcomed *The Golden Notebook* in the 1960s. Ideally suited for this purpose are popular essays of the time, such as the readable survey of American feminism in Shulamith Firestone's *Dialectic of Sex* (16–45) or excerpts from Betty Friedan's classic *The Feminine Mystique* (15–32). Marlene Dixon's "Rise of Women's Liberation" views the movement with special emphasis on the connection between race and sex. Germaine Greer's *Female Eunuch* illustrates the midcentury stereotypes with which *The Golden Notebook*'s first readers were struggling. The widely available anthology by Vivian Gornick and Barbara Moran provides abundant material under one cover, including essays that bridge the gap between life and the literature classroom (e.g., Cynthia Ozick's "Women and Creativity").

So that students of this "crash course" do not infer feminism to be a closed chapter of ages past, it is essential to stress that feminism and social conscience are still alive and necessary as the century draws to a close. Newer studies such as Sylvia Ann Hewlett's *Lesser Life* or Friedan's *Second Stage* demonstrate that most women still suffer from the problems that concerned Anna Wulf and 1960s feminists: stereotyped and exploitative relationships, division of roles between motherhood and the workplace, and lack of support from a (still) largely male-oriented world.

The position occupied by women authors and their works in this male world is reflected by the very diverse readings that have emerged from now over twenty-five years of *Golden Notebook* reception. In these years, feminist criticism was born and has grown up. Many early critiques of the novel, accordingly, reflect the sexist bias of pre-1960s literary criticism, a Victorian tradition that continued unbroken well into the twentieth century. In this male-centered critical approach, women writers were typically belittled for writing about personal problems yet declared unable to write about politics or "real" ideas (Showalter, "Women Writers"; Gilbert and Gubar). Virginia Woolf pointed out that in the condescension toward the personal bias of female literature, a whole value system was at stake: "It is the masculine values that prevail. . . . This is an important book, the critic assumes, because it deals with war. This is an insignificant book because it deals with the feelings of women" (*Room* 77; see also Russ).

The first step toward feminist criticism, then, was a conscious recognition and rejection of traditional male bias in literature (see Ellmann; Ozick). Students' interest in this feminist approach can be engaged, analogously, by demonstrating step-by-step what early masculinist critics did with *The Golden Notebook*. Walking students through a representative prefeminist essay is a back-door approach that reenacts the process of recognition undergone by critics during the crucial years of emerging feminist criticism (1965–75). I select the "Interim View" of F. P. W. McDowell, because his was a fairly audible voice during the early reception of Lessing and because the section on *The Golden Notebook* is brief enough for classroom use. In addition, this article aspires to praise Lessing's achievement while, perversely, often doing just the opposite. The antifeminism in this critical approach can be summarized in three areas:

1. *Naming*. The critic makes a subtle point by stubbornly referring to *Mrs.* Lessing, using the word *Mrs.* over sixty times. Constant reminders of the novelist's supposed marital status also imply that, being a woman, she is not in the same league as "real" authors like (John) Wain or (Lawrence) Durrell (never "Mr. Durrell"). The "Mrs." is a courteous relic of the days when ladies needed special consideration, did not discuss politics—or write books. Students challenged to identify other instances of sexist diction ("the liberal intellectual . . . him" [329]; replacement of "one" with "he" [345]) can be prodded to question the ideological view of the writer.

2. *"Feminine" virtues*. In assessing "Mrs. Lessing," McDowell opens with the question of *women* novelists as distinct from others. Because of the sheer bulk of their work, he generously credits authors like Lessing, Muriel Spark, or Iris Murdoch with "devotion to their craft" (315). Devotion is an emotion rather than an ability (and a craft, one might add, is what women do while men are producing art). These women, McDowell suspects, are manic-compulsive about their writing: "Without the energy . . . and the need which each apparently feels to write continually, perhaps none of them would be

writing at all." Indeed. The emphasis on emotionalism is sustained throughout the article. Examining only the section on *The Golden Notebook*, we
find that it is

> a cross between a standard novel . . . and a *confession*, in which the
> interest is centered on *the writer's attitudes*, values and ideas. . . .
> Mrs. Lessing is to be closely *identified with her heroine* Anna Wulf. . . .
> [The book is] *subjective* in its orientation. . . . Anna Wulf's *inner life*
> is all important. (328; emphasis mine)

Though surely without malicious intent, McDowell adopts the primitive
biographizing of early reviewers and literary gossip columnists who equated
Anna Wulf's experiences with Doris Lessing's private life. He goes on to
imply that, like her author, Anna is a bit too smart for her own good, but
of course her "intellectual difficulties also arise from her sexual frustrations"
(329). These arguments, despite an ostensibly appreciative context, subtly
demote the novel to an emotional woman's product, a presumable confession
of the author's own overintellectualized and sexually frustrated life.

3. *"Masculine" desiderata.* McDowell indicates several times in passing
that he finds *The Golden Notebook*'s "aesthetic" qualities questionable and
its ideas too undisciplined. What is lacking, as he summarizes the book's
drawbacks, is

> a sense of *inevitability* in direction, a *strongly unified* action, and a
> *singleness* of effect. The resources in the novel are more abundant than
> Mrs. Lessing's use of them is *judicious*. (329; emphasis mine)

The novel is "impassioned" but "disorganized" (330), both qualities associated with the feminine stereotype. In other words, Lessing's book is just
not manly enough, since it fails to exhibit the masculine qualities of inev-
itability, strength, single-mindedness, and good judgment.

Early masculinist critiques like the foregoing are instructive *ex negativo*
to apprentice feminist critics. Criticism must not dwell on an author's gender;
it must consciously avoid terms that disparage on the basis of sex. It must
never equate authors with their characters. At the same time, feminist critics
must be very careful not to practice reverse discrimination: their goal must
be, ultimately, not the affirmation of one sex at the expense of the other,
but rather the abolition of sex-specific stereotypes and attitudes that stunt
human interchange. Feminist criticism must demonstrate the role of gender-
based cultural assumptions and patterns in a book's argumentation and its
characters' development, assessing the potency and function of gender as a
political factor in a textual framework. Building on this, it should, ideally,

challenge the whole network of moral and social standards that gender roles reflect: "Feminist criticism is ultimately cultural criticism" (Register 10).

Fortunately for the instructor, Lessing's skillful characterization and her synthetic approach to sexuality as part of a greater network make *The Golden Notebook* ideal for illustrating this critical approach. Anna Wulf is the ideal narrator and, with her habit of intellectually refracting the ideas that make up her notebooks, almost becomes the critic's partner. For Anna Wulf, relationships and politics go hand in hand. When she claims that a novel about emotions should automatically reflect " 'what's real' since the emotions are a function and a product of society" (42), she anticipates a revolutionary insight of the 1960s, by now a somewhat tired cliché: the personal is political. Kate Millett's *Sexual Politics* established this insight as a critical tool, but Anna Wulf, because she consciously uses it as a basis for her reflections, paves the way for a feminist approach to *The Golden Notebook*.

The first step in classroom discussion is to single out individual personae for detailed analysis. An elementary blackboard tabulation illustrates that nearly every character is bound by the stereotypes governing his or her gender. The first male character introduced is Richard Portmain—aggressive, egocentric, and ambitious. The black notebook presents Willi Rodde, a cold and ruthless opportunist. Men like George Hounslow, by contrast, though they "really, very much [need] women" (124), are nonetheless pawns in a system that degrades women. These three figures, united by their exploitation of women and their inability to love deeply and monogamously, coin a self-interested masculine type joined later in the book by men such as Nelson, Paul Tanner, Robert Brun, Cy Maitland, and Saul Green. (An indispensable source for any in-depth discussion of maleness in the novel is Gayle Greene's "Women and Men in Doris Lessing's *The Golden Notebook*: Divided Selves.")

A tabulation of the feminine qualities represented (leaving Anna and Molly aside for the moment) produces similar results—the women are as passive and dependent as the men are aggressive. Many female secondary characters appear as "thirds"—third parties in love-affair triangles. Marion Portmain and the wives of Paul Tanner, Michael, Nelson, Cy Maitland, and De Silva all portray the "trapped housewife" stereotype of the late 1950s (consecutive reading of 26–31, 220–23, 277–82, 322–26, 395–402, 486–94, and 497–504 should precede classroom discussion). Other women who do not fit this group are nonetheless dependent on unsatisfactory sexual relationships: Patricia Brent is a has-been third who ends up accepting the obsequious advances of Dr. West; Maryrose is emotionally damaged forever by the "perfect" but incestuous love of her brother. Just as all male characters in the book share an inability to love, the female characters share an emotional deformation caused by the failure of their male partners to love them.

Of course, these female characters are also guilty of collaboration in this gender-role deadlock: "Lessing's portrayal of woman is making [the point] that woman's complicity in her oppression is at least partly responsible for its continuance" (Greene 292).

Because of Anna's analytical depiction of these characters—and her implicit assertion that these personal things have general significance—the diagnosis of destructive sexual stereotypes already contains a portion of the cure. For the reader is challenged both to relate these highly identifiable types to personal experience and to discard, as does Anna, all that is clearly inadequate. She warns against the "one real sin" of self-delusion about that which is second-rate (649). And contained in this warning is an explicit appeal to the reader: if the second-rate can be correctly named, then the first-rate must exist, if only as a vision, and can at least be sought after. Change, and therefore hope, is possible.

In a second, more detailed discussion of character and role function, the instructor can demonstrate that not only gender stereotypes but also sociopolitical factors predetermine each character. Richard is the embodiment of capitalism, Willi (like other minor male characters) of fanatical communism. Cy Maitland stands for dehumanized medical technology, Paul Tanner for the struggle of social mobility in Britain's highly class-structured society. Perhaps the most striking illustration of the interrelation of sex and politics is George Hounslow. His personal situation, as the white father of an illegitimate son by a black woman, exemplifies the web of sex, race, class, politics, and economics in one poignant subplot (101–53).

The female "thirds" have a class function as well. They are the oppressed proletariat, albeit in a state before the awakening of class consciousness. Lessing places most of them in the suburbs, quietly raising children, papering walls, and reading *Women at Home*. Since Anna and Molly are financially independent, it is these other women who represent the economics of female class oppression. Their dependence on male providers is the precondition to what is today called the feminization of poverty—De Silva's wife provides a representative example (503). The thirds live in double impoverishment: they bear both financial dependence and a chronic dearth of love and affection. The issue of motherhood is a further complicating emotional and economic factor in these women's lives and a highly ambiguous one in all Lessing's works (see Gardiner).

As for Anna and Molly, they have rejected the social convention— marriage—that would make them legal and economic dependents of men. Unlike the trapped housewives, they not only understand the theory of class struggle but also have begun to see gender as a factor in that struggle: "The real revolution is, women against men" (213). In an attempt to sort out life, Anna elevates sex to equal importance with politics, art, "truth," and psychiatry. She also refuses to separate sex from these aspects and insists on women's right to analyze it (214) just as they analyze political events. Even her simple title "Free Women" combines a political category with a gender group. It is no mere coincidence that Anna devotes one well-documented day, which begins and ends with the hectic "housewife's disease" of cooking and caring for others, to the joint enterprise of dealing with her menstrual period and deciding to leave the Communist party (331–68). This demonstrates the complicated intertwinement of female sexuality, domestic duties, and political consciousness. Conversely, Anna's journals typically run aground when she focuses on fragments that are only political (240–49) or only personal (531–41). The red and black notebooks finally end with newspaper clippings, the yellow notebook with fruitless "pastiche"—indicating the futility of isolating political or personal factors from their greater context.

A third phase of textual analysis, focused specifically on Anna, can demonstrate that she actually does very little with her insights into sexual politics. Recognition, not revolution, is her forte (and the reason that readers identified with her en masse). Her behavior is consistently male-oriented and "feminine": she is anxious to please through domestic competence (364; also 605, 640) and reluctant to criticize male behavior; she repeatedly enters alliances with men she despises (70) and is emotionally dependent on males (172, 211, 314, 407). Both she and Molly practice self-denial to "bolster" the male ego (451, 458, 484). Dozens of instances of such feminine behavior patterns can be identified by a close examination of the text in class. Supporting analyses with thorough documentation are available for instructor and student (esp. Morgan, but also Libby; Rapping; and Spacks, "Free Women").

Through this textual analysis students realize, along with Anna, that she is only superficially "free"—that in fact she is bound by the old sexual and cultural norms that fail to produce love or happiness (just as midcentury communism fails to produce justice). Anna Wulf is no less a victim of emotional poverty than Marion and the other betrayed wives; the difference is that she insists on her right to analyze and objectively describe relationships as second-rate and loveless. She insists, further, on her own and every woman's right to search untiringly for better ones (see 143). It was this insistence that incited so many female readers to feminist awareness (see Webb).

Regarding the basic objective of feminist criticism as described above, an assessment of gender-based cultural factors in the book, Lessing's statement is something like this: Sex is deeply political and no less a reflection of human power struggles than are the ideological battles between East and West or black and white. To deny one person happiness is the same as "denying life itself" (*GN* 596). All efforts, male and female, to conform to the sex-role stereotypes of contemporary Western civilization (masculine domination, feminine dependency) end in frustration. Above all, they fail to produce the one key element sorely missed everywhere: the ability to love. *The Golden Notebook* further suggests that emancipation from economic and legal dependency (which Anna has achieved) is not enough to free one from class-related behavior patterns: real change will require long-term "boulder pushing" against one's own and society's habits.

Lessing's perennial optimism—completely undaunted throughout the 1950s and 1960s and, despite her growing disillusionment with many aspects of late twentieth-century life, still potent even in the *Canopus* novels—prevents her from closing *The Golden Notebook* without at least a brief vision of a better alternative. This vision is the interdependence of Anna and Saul Green, as it reaches its culmination in the inner "Golden Notebook." While on the one hand Saul and Anna stand for the greater classes of men and women, locked in a destructive struggle that neither wants and neither can escape, on the other hand they also represent, when they are eventually reconciled, Lessing's hopeful idea of communication and mutual support between the sexes. In the end, Anna feels about Saul "as if he were my brother. . . . it wouldn't matter how we strayed from each other, how far apart we were, we would always be flesh of one flesh, and think each other's thoughts" (641). It is Saul, finally, who literally puts Anna's pen back into her hand and gives her her writer's voice again. Typically for Lessing, who has always contended that men need liberation just as much as women do, Anna and Saul are liberated toward, not from, each other. That their alliance is fragile and short-lived—largely as a result of Saul's neurotic personality —is less important than the fact that it is possible.

Feminism, as Lessing has frequently stated, was not the point of *The Golden Notebook*. The book nevertheless spoke straight from the heart of the contemporary feminist climate in the early 1960s and thus proves that the feminist content of a literary work is, often enough, independent of the author's intentions. Because *The Golden Notebook* grew alongside, not in deliberate collaboration with, the awakening women's movement, it transmits a particularly animated and genuine view of the period's crucial insight—that sex is politics and that both our given sexual and political norms are ripe for revision.

The Golden Notebook's Inner Film

Sharon R. Wilson

Although the projectionist in "The Golden Notebook" section of Lessing's *Golden Notebook* has received some critical attention, no one has explored either the larger role of a film motif or the usefulness of approaching this novel through film theory. The title section of Lessing's *Golden Notebook* self-consciously reflects, and reflects upon, the novel as a whole. Within the section, Anna is not only film writer, actor, director, camera, editor, and projectionist but both film and viewer, within a book in which she is narrator, character, and text. The film motif, with related visual and performance images, is not, however, restricted to the title section: it occurs throughout the novel, frequently in Anna's self-conscious comments on the notebooks or on literature in general and in her dreams or sudden illuminations. Thus, film techniques and analogies provide an intriguing means of discussing Anna and her characters' image making as well as the text's self-conscious theme, imagery, narration, structure, and audience relationship. Film theory, particularly feminist film theory vivid with literary metaphors and parallels, is helpful in approaching Lessing's practice and in assessing its significance. In addition, while students sometimes find the novel's structure and length discouraging and Lessing or her characters' mythology of "real" men, women, and orgasms dated or distancing, they respond to film and literature parallels, which both answer and raise formal questions.

As Roberta Rubenstein said without much elaboration in 1979:

> The analogy of the camera lens can be applied in numerous ways to the form-breaking techniques as well as the themes of the novel. "Vision" is a primary motif, referring not only to Anna Wulf's extended effort to "see" herself as a unified person but also to Lessing's dramatization of many of Anna's psychic realizations through visual images and, ultimately, through the kinds of fusions, overlaps, flashbacks, and superimpositions of time that are more suggestive of film techniques than of the written medium. (*Novelistic Vision* 75–76)

Film in *The Golden Notebook* is more than analogy, however, and like everything else in this ironic novel its use is paradoxical and complex.

Lessing's film motif in *The Golden Notebook* is impossible to demonstrate fully in this short space, but it "runs" in the black, yellow, blue, and golden notebooks. Highly visual scenes and metaphors flow throughout the novel, including the red notebook and the "Free Women" sections; and the overall structure is similarly visual, based on the conjunction of both shape (the square in the circle) and color (see Rubenstein 106–07). In the black notebook, structured by the opposition of Anna's rerun scenes from her Mashopi

115

Hotel days to the *Frontiers of War* material, Anna satirizes movie and television agents who wish to film this novel, imagines them buying artists to destroy creativity and "the real thing" (62–63), and even spontaneously creates a parody script for the Amalgamated Vision company. Her "mental films" (Wilson 33–34, 37–38, 40–43, 48–49) of these experiences are continuously revised as she opposes various "pasts" (of event) and "nows" (of memory, writing, reading, re-visioning), anticipating the projectionist's re-run, reseen films in "The Golden Notebook" section. Ironically, re-creating Maryrose in memory, Anna sees her turn "as in a slow-motion film," recognizes that these moments "all have the absolute assurance of a smile, a look, a gesture, in a painting or a film," and asks whether "the certainty I'm clinging to belongs to the visual arts, and not to the novel, not to the novel at all, which has been claimed by the disintegration and the collapse" (110). The yellow notebook's Ella offers a similar view, even suggesting film's superiority to literature, which is both evasion and "analysis after the event" (228–29).

Near the end of the black notebook, however, Anna dreams that she is seeing a television film, with "real" set and smells, of the Mashopi experiences. Written and directed "by someone else" with the justification that "[i]t doesn't matter what we film, provided we film something," the television play is shot with cameras that become machine-guns; and the director's choice of shots or timing alters the "story" so that Anna watches "Anna, myself, but not as I remembered her," even though her memories are "probably untrue." Not surprisingly, the "name" Anna gives this dream, which erases "the reality," is "total sterility" (524–25). Although both dream theory and textual evidence reveal that Anna plays all the roles in her dreams, as in her fictions, she sometimes feels victimized by the camera, particularly when it seems controlled by a male other.

Susan Sontag's *On Photography* (1977) popularized the notion of the camera as gun, a view expressed in such divergent texts as Margaret Atwood's *Edible Woman* (1969), Christopher Lasch's *Culture of Narcissism* (1978), and Judith Mayne's "Woman at the Keyhole: Women's Cinema and Feminist Criticism" (1981). According to Sontag, "To photograph people is to violate them, by seeing them as they can never see themselves . . . ; it turns people into objects that can be symbolically possessed. Just as the camera is a sublimation of the gun, to photograph someone is a sublimated murder" (14–15). In the feminist film theories of Laura Mulvey, Teresa de Lauretis, Tania Modleski, Linda Williams, and Judith Mayne, it is the female image that the cinematic camera rapes, steals, or otherwise violates. According to Mulvey, "the unconscious of patriarchal society has structured film form. . . . Woman then stands in patriarchal culture as signifier for the male other, . . . [a] bearer of meaning, not maker of meaning." Thus Mulvey calls for the negation of traditional cinematic codes, including the controlling, objectifying gaze of scopophilia, by freeing "the look of the camera into its materiality in time and space and the look of the audience into dialectics, passionate detachment." In other words, the spell of illusion should be broken, preventing distance from the image and thereby denying spectator pleasure (Mulvey, "Visual Pleasure" 6–8, 18). All feminists must share Mulvey's abhorence of a cinematic gaze that is both product of, and vehicle for, oppression of women. But must the camera always be a patriarchal gun?

In later articles Mulvey admits her continued love of film, especially melodrama, and outlines her break with purely negative aesthetics ("Afterthoughts" 12, "Changes" 14). De Lauretis, along with a number of other contemporary feminist critics, considers that the present task of women's cinema is the construction of another frame of reference, a nonsexist cinema "in which the measure of desire is no longer just the male subject" (8). Since the multifaceted Anna of *The Golden Notebook*'s inner film is not only Woman but a woman, she is the kind of subject film theorists seek; she is also a remarkable subject for 1962. Thus, I want to make a bold statement. Despite the camera-gun that threatens dehumanization in the very act of imaging, Lessing, like such filmmakers as Diane Kurys, has already begun constructing the grounds of a female space in the cinema. *The Golden Notebook*'s self-conscious "filming" of itself and its own processes anticipates, in significant ways, the kind of spell-breaking and supposed denial of spectator pleasure for which Mulvey calls. With some differences of medium, Anna's position in the space at the end of the novel—an infinite regress where she is unnamed creator of all we have read and seen, including herself as camera, projectionist, screen image, and spectator—also anticipates de Lauretis: "The question then is how to reconstruct or organize vision from the 'impossible' place of the female spectator between the look of the camera and the image on the screen, and how to represent the terms of her double identification in the process of looking at her looking" (69). Perhaps Lessing's foregrounding of literary and selected cinematic "codes" and techniques (image, narration, structure, flashback, close-up, long shot, montage, framing, and the illusion of reality) can even be useful in moving feminist cinema from theory to further action.

Judith Mayne, however, is much less optimistic. Her brief discussion of *The Golden Notebook*'s camera-gun and projectionist is provocative if somewhat misleading. Distinguishing women's separate literary tradition from their relative invisibility in cinema, she alludes to the relation Lessing draws between female identity and artistic production: in the cinema, "the woman is the viewer, man the projectionist, and the whole viewing process a form of control and domination. . . . Lessing's cinematic metaphor is informed by an insight into the patriarchal nature of the relation of projectionist to

screen, viewer to image." The cinematic camera is "eye, gun . . . *and* penis."
As Mayne recognizes, however, even referencing films of Michelle Citron
and Sally Potter, Lessing's cinematic metaphor is part of Anna's attempt to
"distill and clarify experience. . . . The films represent what Anna calls her
'burden of recreating order out of the chaos' " (53–54). Thus, Mayne's equa-
tion of Anna with the dominated female spectator seems simplistic.

Anna's projectionist clearly represents a controlling part of *Anna*: her
"inner conscience or critic," the "disinterested personality" who "saved [her]
from disintegration" by saying that she must look at "scenes" from her life
"straight" (*GN* 621, 616). As *The Children of Violence, Briefing for a Descent
into Hell, The Memoirs of a Survivor*, and *Canopus in Argos* suggest, however, disintegration, or "breaking down," may be necessary to the creative
order Anna seeks, an order lying beyond a "straight" vision. The projectionist
part of Anna's personality, her "straight" vision, can take her only to the
point of "illumination" where "words, patterns, order, dissolve": speculating
that music, a row of asterisks, or a symbol such as the circle or square might
communicate better than words, an intuitive or "crooked" Anna turns off
the projector (633–35).

Despite the ultimately healing function of film, the projectionist is a paradoxical figure. Anna's masculinization and naming of this often malicious
and abusive part of herself are revealing. The Saul Green of the blue notebook, a screenwriter who says he left Hollywood because "there wasn't
anybody left in it who was capable of believing that a writer would refuse
money rather than have a bad film made," sometimes performs as camera-
gun as well as agent-star: he assaults Anna with a brutal sexual gaze, strikes
macho film poses, and shoots the word *I* at her "like bullets from a machine
gun" (552, 556). Projected into the projectionist, "he" reminds us of numerous male characters (Nelson of the blue notebook, Milt of the final "Free
Women" section) in this and other Lessing books. In both blue and golden
notebooks, however, Saul, like Anna, is multiple. He is whining or delinquent child, father, friend, enemy, lover, double, and foil: he is archetypal
character (object as well as subject) in Anna's text. "Naming" one part of
Anna "Saul" could be explained in reference to androgyny or a Jungian
system; and it does highlight Anna and Saul's mutual "projection" of moods
and personalities in the "Golden Notebook," culminating in the fictive beginnings the authors write for each other. In relation to feminist film theory,
however, if the male projectionist reveals the character Anna's internalization
of patriarchal codes, he also illuminates Lessing and the author Anna's ironic
foregrounding of them.

Because of this foregrounding, and because the author Anna successfully
orders her disintegrated inner stories and films by creating and publishing
the novel we read, film in *The Golden Notebook* signifies something other

than control and domination. As de Lauretis and Modleski admit, feminist film theory has been overrestrictive in assessing both cinematic possibilities of narrative and visual pleasure and the female spectator's position. Despite Mayne's limited reading of Lessing's projectionist, she concludes paradoxically by choosing the projector as "an appropriate figure for the tasks of feminist criticism. Through projection, individual frames of celluloid are shot through with light and acquire the semblance of continuity" (63–64). As in *The Edible Woman* and other texts by Margaret Atwood, Margaret Laurence, and Anne Hébert, camera and film images in *The Golden Notebook* may be positive as well as negative. If cameras and film "foster and record fragmentation, sometimes deceiving with false power and certainty, they may also function as lenses which distill and focus experience, facilitating a self-discovery which transcends mere 'self-surveillance' as well as social roles and games" (Wilson 32).

The Anna who watches films of her life cannot be categorized masochistic spectator or spectacle, voyeur, exhibitionist, or silenced victim (see L. Williams 91–92); and neither can we who sit beside as well as opposite her. If she views "footage" in which she plays the hardly visible leader's girlfriend, the "lady writer," the betrayed woman, and a "young mother playing with her little girl," she also sees/creates long shots of "herself" as characters in her intertexts and recognizes certain film images or scenes as "fantasies common to a certain kind of person now. . . . [they were] what bound people, of a certain kind, unknown to each other as individuals, together" (596–97). Anna's self-conscious vision, both distancing and intuitive, breaks the illusion of reality, violating and foregrounding both fiction and cinematic codes without, I think, destroying pleasure. Sometimes disrupting our reading/viewing as she zooms in on "technical hitches" where text is written or "shot badly," she does close-ups, even parodies, of "brickwork" (characterization, theme, dialogue, timing, lighting, structure) in her texts within a text (227, 476, 536, 610, 617, 637). By offering multiple focuses, filters, and perspectives, *The Golden Notebook* begins to liberate the woman artist and generate a charged textual space for "mutual gazing" (Gentile 80), a place inclusive of women, where images might move and speak without placing, encasing, or displacing women.

We *see* only the mirrored reflections of the Anna who has been able to merge the different colors and identities and create one book, *The Golden Notebook*, which she is. Thus, we are left with some unresolved questions. Could the work be filmed, and, if so, would the film necessarily leave a space to suggest Anna's final presence? Given cinema's transformation of a real actress into a screen image unable to return our gazes, is cinema capable of showing a "real woman" without making her a spectacle, thereby dehumanizing her? Despite the differences in literary and cinematic imaging, both women's literature (*The Handmaid's Tale*) and film (*Entre Nous*) usually, perhaps wisely, deny vision of the "whole" woman. Considering literature and cinema's historic enslavement of the female image, once "seen," could she still become? As Gentile and others argue, however, when the female viewer addresses the process of identification—looks at her own looking (81, 84), as, in varying degrees, Lina Wertmüller's *Night Full of Rain*, Yvonne Rainer's *Film about a Woman Who . . .* , and *The Golden Notebook* cause us to do—cinema and literature can become both interactive and authentic.

The film metaphor in *The Golden Notebook* is, finally, a literary metaphor, realized for spectators on a page instead of a screen. Paradoxically, Lessing does say with words what cannot be said in words but can be said only in author-narrator-text-audience interaction. To appreciate the novel with its many Annas, *The Golden Notebook* demands that we be our own projectionists, dissolving text to rerun and resee, as Anna does, individual shots and sequences without full meaning until all have been viewed and then projected into a new, implied coherence. Female spectator-readers are actively engaged in this montage, directing and, who knows, starring in their own versions of *The Golden Notebook*. Lessing's antinovel dismantles and reintegrates both literature and cinema, showing not cinema's superiority to fiction (or the opposite) but the possibilities of a disintegrated form in a disintegrating society.

"Where words, patterns, order, dissolve": *The Golden Notebook* as Fugue

Sandra Brown

Quartered and color coded, *The Golden Notebook* has no real beginning, middle, or end. There appear to be several storytellers. To deal with this stylistic departure from Doris Lessing's previous work, a reader tries to connect the separate parts of the story, figure out the novel's message, and identify the "real" narrator. The novel can vex readers intent on listening for a sign of the familiar small, personal voice, for in a novel "where words, patterns, order, dissolve" (633), it is not easily found.

The Golden Notebook instead seems to be an anthology of the collected writings of Anna Wulf. Lessing's systematic rotation of at least four narrative voices, as effective as a trick with mirrors, is directly responsible for her illusory disappearance. The divided episodes are cycled until they synthesize or syncretize in a compressed section followed by a final episode—the "analysis after the event" (228). Her scaffold is camouflaged, however, by the difficult reading itself, the ambiguity surrounding Anna's recovery (Does she become whole and write again? Is her golden notebook the new fictional mode she seeks?), and by Lessing's description of her spontaneity in composing: "keeping the plan of it in my head I wrote it from start to end, consecutively" (x).

It is important to recognize that Lessing does not share Anna's dilemma, although she and her protagonist are both concerned about the artistic representation in writing of life as it is lived. Anna writes:

> Words. Words. I play with words, hoping that some combination, even a chance combination, will say what I want. Perhaps better with music? But music attacks my inner ear like an antagonist, it's not my world. (633)

Culminating her despair over war, social injustice, and the loss of love, the semiotic problem drives her mad. Ironically, she verbalizes but does not see the clue to its solution. Anna's half-formed ideas prompt the question, Does Lessing see? It would appear that she does: for however unintentional, however distinctly conceived, she does craft a musiclike form to shape her world of the novel, taking it well beyond the traditional realm of words, patterns, order.

Far from the "chance combination" Anna hopes for, Lessing's careful arrangement of Anna's separate voices produces a form similar to a fugue. Interestingly, the jazz composer Gerry Mulligan, whose plaintive music is one of the last memories entered in Anna's blue notebook (607), has translated his interpretation of Lessing's contrapuntal patterns into a jazz composition entitled "Golden Notebooks." Reviewing his album, Susan Bourgeois points to his use of

> a very traditional relatively simple musical form, that [is] found in fugues and madrigals, for instance, in which there is a statement of theme, variation and development of theme, and return to the original statement.   (12)

But Lessing's form can hardly be considered simple. Anna's "doodlings, scattered musical symbols, treble signs that shifted into the & sign and back again" (56), conceived on "an old-fashioned music stool" (55, 476), hint at the need for closer analysis. Such a study provides not only an explanation of the book's structure but also illumination regarding its message and recognition of the full extent of Lessing's artistic vision.

The techniques of alternation, restatement, and reiteration of themes, found in contrapuntal music composition, in general can be applied to the writing of poetry and prose. Yet, more detailed contrapuntal structures used in *The Golden Notebook* are ordinarily specific to the writing of music only. Working definitions of such musical devices are necessary to make the analogy to prose and to illustrate their uses in discussing narrative voice in the novel.

The first of these is *imitation*. After one voice begins the melody, the second imitates it (as in "Row, row, row your boat"). On the simplest level, Ella imitates Anna; Paul imitates Michael. A *canon* is merely a more complex form of imitation. Since the imitations of Lessing-Anna are more complex than "Row, row, row your boat," it is fitting to speak of her forms as canons.

A contrapuntal device known as *inversion* is sometimes used for canons. The second voice moves by the same intervals (tones) as the first, but in the opposite direction. Such canons are known as *mirror canons*. In musical theory, the first voice moves upward in a given pattern (at given intervals); the second voice imitates the first by moving downward at the same intervals, and so on. Where Anna "cures" Saul by absorbing his illness, Milt, his counterpart, is Anna's healer. Ripping down her newspaper clippings, he saves her from the brink of madness:

> "Thank you for taking that nonsense off my walls. Thank you. Another few days and I really would have gone around the bend."
>   ". . . there's one thing I'm good at, seeing someone in trouble and knowing what strong measures to take."   (662)

When a melody is played backward, the procedure is known as *retrograde motion*. Canons that use this procedure are known as *cancrizans* or *crab canons*. In the yellow notebook's entry (531–41) accompanying her diary, or chronicle, in the blue notebook (542–607), Anna lists nineteen synopses of possible short stories based on her relationship with Saul. This listing, placed as it is before the fully described life situation, is precisely a cancrizan, coming as it does before the fact. To analyze Anna's projection of life into the fictional mode, one must read the sequence backward.

The device by which a melody is imitated by a slower, second voice is known as *augmentation*. Moving proportionately in note values twice as long as the first, the lower, second voice creates what one musicologist calls a "hare and tortoise situation" (Miller 105). "Free Women" succinctly tells the story of Anna Wulf, augmented by the four notebooks, which move in a "lower voice," perhaps a more serious voice, certainly a more detailed, emotional voice, coming closer to photographic realism; in length slightly more than twice that of the "Free Women" sections. The hare-and-tortoise situation works as well allegorically in describing the effect in Lessing's prose structure; the notebooks, merged at last as "The Golden Notebook" (obviously, the tortoise), win the race, coming as they do before the conclusion of "Free Women." Saul and Anna part; that curtain closes. But Anna must still finish Anna and Milt's race, which she accomplishes in the fifth and final chapter of "Free Women" (647–66). In this version, Molly and Anna part when Molly marries, ringing down the second and final curtain with a securely felt *coda* (musically, an independent concluding passage).

In the *double canon*, two different melodies move simultaneously, each being imitated canonically by still another voice, with four parts in all. The black and red notebooks deal with public life: publishing and politics. The two are closely related, when Anna's early experiences with the Communist party echo in *Frontiers of War*. Anna's yellow notebook is the dramatization of the blue, her true personal life.

The most important contrapuntal form is the *fugue*, the term originating from the Latin *fuga*, meaning flight. It is based on the imitation of a short theme called the *subject*, which is easily recognizable. In fugues the number of voices may be three or more, but the subject is announced, or introduced, by one voice alone (the *dux*). A second voice (the *comes*) then states the theme a fifth scale degree higher, or a fourth lower. This is called the *answer*. A third voice then comes in with the subject, a fourth with the answer, and so on until all the parts have made their entries. While the subject or the answer is being stated, the voice or voices that have already entered continue with other counterpoint. The counterpoint that appears consistently with the subject or answer, after the first statement of the subject by itself (Anna is both the author and subject of her writings), is called the *countersubject*. The subject is stated recurrently in one voice after another throughout the fugue. Passages during which the subject is not being stated are called *episodes*.

The Golden Notebook may properly be described as a flight of ideas; the subject—the experiences and impressions of a single woman in her twenties living in South Africa and later as a thirty-two-year-old divorced mother living in London—is "imitated" in *Frontiers of War* and "The Shadow of the Third," as well as in "Free Women" and "The Golden Notebook," which are analogous to the alternated "answer." Each is "higher" or "lower," that is, with modulation or variations on a theme, but repeats the real life experiences. In addition, the four notebooks fit the definition for the comes in that they are different aspects of Anna's self. Each voice makes its entry separately. The consecutive divisions signal the continuation of counterpoint: Anna writes of her life as she lives it but also records recurring thoughts and dreams of her earlier experiences at the Mashopi Hotel. In a complex marbling of themes, one voice after another recurrently states the subject; yet each notebook, in its insistently unallied category, acts as an episode in separating the ongoing unity ("Free Women"). The musicologist Donald Tovey claims, however, that although episodes may be "conspicuously" independent, in the main they "are usually developed from the material of the subject and countersubjects" (37). This is most certainly true in *The Golden Notebook*. Further, we may consider the chapters of "Free Women" to constitute the episodes, with the notebooks acting as the statement of the subject. Since "fugue is a texture the rules of which do not suffice to determine the shape of the composition as a whole" and since "schemes . . . which legislate for the shape are pedagogic fictions" (Tovey 36–37), we are safe in applying the contrapuntal discipline to *The Golden Notebook* in a somewhat flexible manner.

Where does "The Golden Notebook" come in? Not surprisingly, there is a device in fugue writing known as the *stretto*. It is a passage in which various strands of subject, answer, and countersubject come together in an intense and passionate fusion of voices. Aaron Copland describes it this way:

> A stretto in a fugue is optional, but when present it is usually found just before the final cadence. Stretto is the name given a species of imitation in which the separate parts enter so immediately one after another that an impression of toppling voices is obtained. (98)

Tovey states, "Stretto is the overlapping of subject and answer. A 'stretto maestrale' is one in which the subject survives the overlapping" (37). Conforming utterly to this fugal device, "The Golden Notebook" opens with a description of the dark:

> It is so dark in this flat, so dark, it is as if darkness were the shape of cold. I went through the flat turning on light everywhere, the dark retreated to outside the windows, a cold shape trying to press its way in. (611)

The passage harks back to the opening of the black notebook, the first of the four:

> black
>   dark, it is so dark
>   it is dark
>   there is a kind of darkness here. (56)

Two entries and two years after the opening description, a title for the black notebook, announced in capital letters, appears: "*THE DARK*" (57).

The "overlapping" continues in the language Anna uses to describe the loathsome feelings she has for her body:

> I sat on my bed and I looked at my thin white legs and my thin white arms, and at my breasts. My wet sticky centre seemed disgusting, and when I saw my breasts all I could think of was how they were when they were full of milk, and instead of this being pleasurable, it was revolting. (612)

The obnoxious words derive from Ivor and Ronnie's conversation, heard earlier:

> 'Fat buttocky cows . . .' That was Ivor's voice, and he added an obscene noise. Then Ronnie's voice: 'Sagging sweaty breasts . . .' And he made the sound of vomiting. (406)

Anna's sense of unreality and her symbolic dream (613–16) repeat her sessions with Mother Sugar; the dream itself mirrors her relationship with Saul (the tiger) caged in her flat, while her life whirls by as a film shown by a projectionist (Saul again). Toward the end of the notebook, Anna feels the urge to write again and resurrect Ella ("she would be wearing different clothes" [637]), whom she had not thought of in a long time. The "subject survives the overlapping" as "The Golden Notebook" ends with the voice of the dux emerging from the maelstrom, or fusion of "toppling voices."

The independence of chapter 5 of "Free Women," requisite for a coda, is due to its being unallied with any diary, or notebook, to back it up. The trusted notebooks are closed; we have no means of checking fiction against fact. Aside from its conformity to the coda, the section is necessary to prove that Anna finished her second novel—and its completion parallels the ending of a fugue. By sending the reader back to the beginning (639), she is sending us to this end. This fugue is complete.

Although the fugue is manifest in no other single work Lessing has written, its clear outline in *The Golden Notebook* symbolizes the recursiveness of major themes throughout her novelistic canon: a return to the center of consciousness, to a place of renewal, to a place of artistic renaissance. Further, *The Golden Notebook*, marking a critical phase in Lessing's expanding artistic vision, is paradigmatic of her future emphasis on multiple narrative voices that elude identification as the author's persona.

John Dewey has pointed to the common substance of art, and it is in this sense that I find the fugal structure a useful analogy in explaining to students Lessing's complex interweaving of narrative voice in *The Golden Notebook*. In speaking of accent and interval, two qualities similarly handled in fugue composition and *The Golden Notebook*'s structure, Dewey states:

> They are determined by the necessity of maintaining the relations that bind parts into a whole. But also without these elements, parts would be a jumble, running aimlessly into one another; they would lack the demarcation that individualizes. In music or verse there would be meaningless lapses. (203)

Although Lessing's novel intends to reproduce the chaos of reality, its form is far from a "jumble"; by individualizing each of Anna's voices, Lessing defines the whole: the woman and the modern world. The latter becomes unified in the clarified perspective of the former.

But Anna's new fictional mode, the fusion and inclusion of all volumes in her collection, emblematic of her recovery, is not the fugue. Only Lessing crafts Anna's quaternion into the profoundly complex literary form paralleling music's most intricate structure. But somehow, for discovering a way to dissolve the old patterns, the old order of words, Lessing is in Anna's debt.

The Golden Notebook:
A Challenge to the Teaching Establishment

Katherine Fishburn

Ever since 1971, when Doris Lessing published the preface to *The Golden Notebook*, those of us who teach this novel have found ourselves in an awkward pedagogical position. The problem, of course, is that in the preface Lessing specifically advises her readers to experience the book on their own without any form of outside interference. In so doing, she has deprived us of the credibility we need in order to maintain our authority in the classroom. For how could we presume to explain the text if we so shamelessly contravene the author's wishes about how it should be read? Because Lessing insists on the sanctity of the reader-text relation, if we teach her book—no matter what kind of critical context we place it in—we seem set on committing an unforgivable act of bad faith. To avoid this offense, we would appear to be left with nothing to do except make the reading assignment in the first place. In short, Lessing's preface makes our lives extremely difficult. If under these adverse circumstances we decide to teach her novel anyway, we had better know what we are doing and be prepared for the consequences. For in teaching *The Golden Notebook* we will be biting the institutional hand that feeds us.

Although Lessing does not address her preface only to our students, she does seem to have gone out of her way to warn them not to listen to us. She has apparently concluded that Western educational systems are responsible for most of the social ills plaguing the world today. Because she is critical of how and what the schools teach, she wants to be able to speak directly to her readers through her fiction—without the voice of institutional authority somehow perverting her message. If her work is taught in schools, the chances are good that somebody is telling her readers what her books mean. To cast doubt on our "official" interpretations, therefore, she tells students ahead of time to ignore what we say. In other words, she has written a preface that has the same iconoclastic purpose as the novel it accompanies. Although we may not like it, the preface to *The Golden Notebook* is *supposed* to make us teachers uncomfortable. For part of Lessing's pedagogical strategy is to educate those who would read her work and those who would teach it. What first looks like an essay written for student-readers, therefore, is also an essay written for us, her student-teachers. For Lessing seems to be openly challenging us to come up with a way of talking about her fiction that complements her purpose in writing. The paramount question she raises in our minds, in response to this challenge, has to do with whether we are capable of teaching her fiction without institutionalizing it. That is, she asks us if we can teach *The Golden Notebook* without ipso facto imposing a form and meaning on it that it does not have—if we can teach her novel as process and not as doctrine. In challenging us so openly, she really asks us if we dare teach this novel at all. In this essay, I meet this challenge by arguing that *The Golden Notebook* is a book eminently suited—if not designed— for teaching.

Before addressing the basic problem of this paper, however, I think it pertinent to raise the question of why Lessing so mistrusts teachers and critics. Some of the reasons she alludes to in the preface itself, where she refers to what she considers to have been misreadings of her novel. She was upset by these misreadings, she says, because, like other authors, she longs for the "perfect critic," the author's alter ego, "that other self more intelligent than oneself who has seen what one is reaching for, and who judges you only by whether you have matched up to your aim or not" (xv). Although all novelists are plagued by critical obtuseness, Lessing seems particularly stung to be so misunderstood in this novel. She does not blame the reviewers directly, however; rather, she goes to the heart of the problem and blames the schools these reviewers have attended. Because schools are by and large institutions that describe the world for us, in Lessing's opinion they turn out readers who have been trained to doubt their own judgment. Instead of helping students become more open-minded and sympathetic readers, the schools, she says, train them "in the opposite direction" (xv). In so doing, the schools turn out critics who are especially ill-suited to understand her work, which above all requires of its readers a combination of skepticism and intellectual inquiry. Is it any wonder she sees the schools' failure in a personal light? Compounding her disillusionment is the fact that Lessing herself is preeminently a teacher, one whose vision forces her to work outside and in opposition to the educational system. If we are going to accept her challenge and teach *The Golden Notebook*, therefore, we must use it as it was intended to be used: as a text designed to transform our perceptions of the world. That is to say, we as teachers must understand that when we teach Doris Lessing's fiction, we are engaging in a political activity.

It is, of course, arguable that whenever we teach any literature, we are engaged in a political activity, either in supporting or subverting the status quo. Certainly, both language and literature are themselves invaluable repositories of cultural and political thought. It can even be argued, as Peter Berger and Thomas Luckmann have, that language is the single most powerful socializing agent available to any culture in the transmission of its ideas from generation to generation (*Social Construction* 37). In most cultures, including our own, schoolteachers are responsible for accomplishing this mission of socialization. Thus Lessing is not incorrect in claiming that students in school "are in the process of being indoctrinated" (xvii). This statement, of course, returns us to her distrust of teachers and provides us with perhaps our best explanation of why she prefers her work not be taught.

Which is simply this: because she is writing literature that would subvert the system, she does not want her work taught by those whose job is to maintain it.

But if language and literature are used by society to socialize its members and control its deviants, they can also be used by those like Lessing herself who would transform society. Her own method of teaching is an indirect one adapted from Sufi teaching stories. Confronting readers with a series of contradictions and paradoxes that elude conventional logic, Lessing challenges us to an intellectual engagement with her text. Like the Sufi masters she emulates, she hopes to subvert our worldview and our certainties by posing us difficult questions about the nature of reality. For, as Judith Stitzel eloquently demonstrates, it is not doctrine that interests Lessing but thinking (502). In other words, the goal of all Lessing's fiction is to enhance our ability to see beyond ourselves by involving us in an intellectual debate with the text itself. In *The Golden Notebook* this strategy helps to account for the novel's unusual structure through which she hopes to teach readers how to escape institutionalized thought. She accomplishes this less by what she says to her readers than by what she does with them. That is, taking her cue from the Sufis, she has constructed a novel whose very shape makes "a wordless statement" about contemporary society and the conventional novel itself (*GN* xiv). What the shape of her text states is that the complexities and uncertainties of twentieth-century life can no longer be accommodated by the conventional novel, as evidenced by the "Free Women" sections. Of all the sections, these are by far the most orderly versions of what happens to Anna Wulf. But because they do not reflect the anguish of her fragmentation, they are ultimately unsatisfactory accounts of her life.

If they are inadequate as psychological truth, the "Free Women" sections do illustrate the dangers of submitting to a fatal nostalgia for meaning and order, a nostalgia that Lessing apparently both fears and desires. It is a nostalgia that pervades all her fiction and one that Albert Camus describes in *The Myth of Sisyphus* as a "nostalgia for unity, that appetite for the absolute," which he finds characteristic of the "human drama" in its perennial longing for understanding and order (13). This longing for form is so central to the human experience that, according to Camus, it is tempting to see in others' lives "a coherence and unity which they cannot have in reality, but which seem evident to the spectator" (*Rebel* 261). The desire for unity seems to describe the difficulty that Anna has in perceiving her own life, whether she is looking back on it, as in the black notebook's account of her African experiences, or trying to record it synchronically, as in the blue notebook's account of her daily activities. To her dismay, she realizes that in giving her life shape and meaning, whether as fact or as fiction, she is, by definition, falsifying it. She is perhaps most aware of this effect when she remarks at the end of the first installment of the yellow notebook that she has written the story of Paul and Ella not the way they originally experienced it but "in terms of analysis of the laws of dissolution of the relationship" between them (227). In other words, knowing how the relationship ends affects how she describes its beginnings.

In each of her four notebooks and in the frame tale, Anna presents separate views of herself, discrete roles she plays in her encounters with a troublesome world. In these sections, she demonstrates her own and the world's fragmentation. But in *The Golden Notebook* Anna demonstrates the integration of these same fragments. This integration is made possible by Anna's breakdown in the inner "Golden Notebook," but it is anticipated in the notebooks themselves, as she begins to confuse them in her own mind. The paradox in this novel, of course, is that its wholeness is composed of fragments that have been experienced by Anna precisely as fragments and not as part of a meaningful whole. And because a first reading is basically a linear activity, we too initially experience only the fragmentation of Anna's life. Only after we have read the novel and can look back on it, can we begin to see the unity the fragments constitute. At this point, we reflect and even repeat what Anna herself has done in assembling the book.

By composing the text out of fragments, however, Anna has not only commented on her own life, she has also given us an extended metaphor that incorporates herself, the world, and the novel. As other critics like Roberta Rubenstein ("Lessing's *The Golden Notebook*") and Mary Ann Singleton have ably pointed out, no one part of *The Golden Notebook* contains the "truth" or represents reality per se. Instead, each of the major sections provides a metaphor for all the others (see Carnes for another view of metaphor). That is, in a metaphorical sense, "Free Women" is the black notebook is the red notebook is the yellow notebook is the blue notebook is the "The Golden Notebook." In discussing the characteristics of metaphor, Max Black maintains that when we say A is B, we are saying something about A (it is B) and simultaneously something about B (it is A) (25–47). Thus if Anna is Ella, Ella is also Anna. Therefore, it follows that Anna is no more real than Ella, and Ella is no more fictional than Anna (wherever Anna appears). Because there is no distinction between fiction and reality in this novel, it is, as Patricia Waugh notes, a classic example of metafictional or self-conscious writing (74–77).

If we cannot locate a consistent reality base in this novel, we also have no internally consistent picture of Anna-Ella herself. Instead, we are supplied with a series of alternative routes through one woman's psyche. Although we might be tempted to take the routes one at a time to their ends, the book simply will not allow it. The structure of the novel forces us to switch tracks so often that we become confused over what we have encountered where. Lessing complicates the picture further by peppering the narrative with conflicting information, apparently calculated to remind us once again that there is no ultimate reality either inside or outside the text. This destruction of everyday reality seems to have been one of Lessing's major reasons for writing *The Golden Notebook* the way she did. For in destroying our old realities, she can introduce us to new ones that challenge some of our most deeply held convictions about the nature of the universe. Like other metafiction, the text itself functions as an attack on our conventional picture of the world as an orderly and, finally, comprehensible place. Through the metaphor of Lessing's fiction, we learn that the meaning of the world will do nothing but elude us if we try to pin it down—either by institutionalizing, fictionalizing, or labeling it. In short, we can only experience the world. We cannot explain it.

In teaching Doris Lessing, therefore, we state, at least implicitly, that there are several ways of looking at the world, that no one social, religious, or political institution has a monopoly on truth. In teaching Lessing, we mediate between the closed world of contemporary society and the open world of her fiction. Teaching her novel as it was meant to be taught, we can help guide our students to the strange and unexpected image of wholeness that lies at the center of her writing. In effect, in teaching her, we are exchanging, if only briefly, our version of reality for her vision of reality. What we are given, then, is the opportunity to replace the teaching of dogma with the teaching of process. That is, rather than teaching our students what to think, we are teaching them how to think. Rather than indoctrinating them, we are educating them in the original sense of leading them out of themselves and the world they know.

But these glorious achievements will only come about if we avoid the temptation to canonize her. Teaching her must be an act of subversion that denies the power of institutions—even literary ones—to describe the world for us. *The Golden Notebook* begs to be taught, but only on its own terms. If we are to respect Lessing's wishes and her text, therefore, we cannot do less than free ourselves from the same constraints she has freed herself from. For most of us this means abandoning safe critical havens and habits and lighting out for new territory. What she asks of us is not impossible, but it is surely difficult. It is a challenge not everyone can meet.

Teach her only if you dare.

SURVEY PARTICIPANTS

The following scholars and teachers of Lessing generously agreed to participate in the survey of approaches to teaching *The Golden Notebook* that preceded the preparation of this volume. Without their invaluable assistance and generous support, the volume would not have been possible.

Norma Barricelli, Riverside City College; Jane Colville Betts, University of Wisconsin, Eau Claire; Sandra Brown, Ocean County College; Selma Burkom, San Jose State University; Lorelei Cederstrom, Brandon University, Canada; Jonathan Culler, Cornell University; Rachel Blau DuPlessis, Temple University; Katherine Fishburn, Michigan State University; Judith Kegan Gardiner, University of Illinois, Chicago; James Gindin, University of Michigan, Ann Arbor; Gayle Greene, Scripps College; Andrew Gurr, University of Reading, England; Sharon Hileman, Sul Ross State University; Molly Hite, Cornell University; Joseph Hynes, University of Oregon; Nicole Ward Jouve, York University, England; Mona Knapp, University of Utah; Marjorie Lightfoot, Arizona State University; Alice Markow, West Chester University; Jean Pickering, California State University, Fresno; Annis Pratt, University of Wisconsin, Madison; Maria Christina Rodrigues, Universidad Interamericana, Puerto Rico; Susan Jean Rosowski, University of Nebraska, Lincoln; Roberta Rubenstein, American University; Ruth Saxton, Mills College; Paul Schlueter, Easton, Pennsylvania; Patrocinio Schweickart, University of New Hampshire, Durham; Elaine Showalter, Princeton University; Claire Sprague, New York University; Frederick C. Stern, University of Illinois, Chicago; Catharine R. Stimpson, Rutgers University, New Brunswick; Virginia Tiger, Rutgers University, Newark; Sharon R. Wilson, University of Northern California.

WORKS CITED

Abel, Elizabeth. "*The Golden Notebook*: 'Female Writing' and 'The Great Tradition.' " Sprague and Tiger 101–07.

Alter, Robert. *Partial Magic: The Novel as a Self-Conscious Genre*. Berkeley: U of California P, 1975.

Axelrod, Steven Gould. "Teaching *Moby-Dick* to Non–English Majors." Bickman 66–74.

Barber, James. *Rhodesia: The Road to Rebellion*. London: Methuen, 1977.

Barth, John. *The Friday Book: Essays and Other Nonfiction*. New York: Putnam's, 1984.

Beauvoir, Simone de. *The Second Sex*. 1949. Trans. H. M. Parshley. 1953. New York: Bantam, 1967.

Beck, Anthony. "Doris Lessing and the Colonial Experience." *Journal of Commonwealth Literature* 19 (1984): 64–73.

Berger, Peter L., and Thomas Luckmann. *The Social Construction of Reality: A Treatise in the Sociology of Knowledge*. 1966. Garden City: Anchor, 1967.

Berkowitz, Peggy, et al. "Reports: Lessing in North America, March-April, 1984." *Doris Lessing Newsletter* 8.2 (1984): 5.

Bertelsen, Eve, ed. *Doris Lessing*. Johannesburg: McGraw, 1985.

Bickman, Martin, ed. *Approaches to Teaching Melville's* Moby-Dick. New York: MLA, 1985.

Black, Hugo. Dissent in Barenblatt v. United States of America. 35 US (1959).

Black, Max. *Models and Metaphors: Studies in Language and Philosophy*. Ithaca: Cornell UP, 1962.

Blake, Robert. *A History of Rhodesia*. London: Methuen, 1977.

Boffa, Giuseppa. *Inside the Khrushchev Era*. Trans. Carl Marzani. New York: Marzani, 1959.

Booth, Wayne. *The Rhetoric of Fiction*. Chicago: U of Chicago P, 1961.

Bourgeois, Susan. " 'Golden Notebooks': Patterns in *The Golden Notebook*." Rev. of "Golden Notebooks," by Gerry Mulligan. *Doris Lessing Newsletter* 3.2 (1979): 5.

Brockbank, Philip. "Joyce and Literary Tradition: Language Living, Dead and Resurrected, from Genesis to Guinesses." McCormack and Stead 166–84.

Broderick, Catherine. "Doris Lessing in Japan." *Doris Lessing Newsletter* 7.1 (1983): 13.

Brooks, Ellen W. "The Image of Women in Lessing's *The Golden Notebook*." *Critique* 15 (1973): 101–10.

Brooks, Van Wyck. "On Creating a Usable Past." *Dial* 64 (1918): 337–41.

Bruss, Elizabeth. *Autobiographical Acts*. Baltimore: Johns Hopkins UP, 1976.

Camus, Albert. *The Myth of Sisyphus and Other Essays*. 1955. Trans. Justin O'Brien. New York: Knopf, 1964.

———. *The Rebel: An Essay on Man in Revolt*. Trans. Anthony Bower. 1951. New York: Vintage, 1956.

Carey, Alfred Augustine. "Doris Lessing: The Search for Reality. A Study of the Major Themes in Her Novels." Diss. U of Wisconsin, 1965.

Carey, John L. "Art and Reality in *The Golden Notebook*." *Contemporary Literature* 14 (1973): 437–56. Rpt. in Pratt and Dembo 20–39.

Carnes, Valerie. " 'Chaos, That's the Point': Art as Metaphor in Doris Lessing's *The Golden Notebook*." *World Literature Written in English* 15 (1976): 17–28.

Cederstrom, Lorelei. "The Process of Individuation in *The Golden Notebook*." *Gradiva* 2 (1979): 41–54.

Chasseguet-Smirgel, Janine. "Feminine Guilt and the Oedipus Complex." *Female Sexuality: New Psychoanalytic Views*. By Chasseguet-Smirgel et al. Ann Arbor: U of Michigan P, 1970. 94–134.

Chennells, Anthony. "Doris Lessing and the Rhodesian Settler Novel." Bertelsen 31–44.

Copland, Aaron. *What to Listen For in Music*. 1953. New York: McGraw, 1977.

Culler, Jonathan. "Comparative Literature and the Pieties." *Profession 86* (1986): 30–32.

de Lauretis, Teresa. *Alice Doesn't: Feminism, Semiotics, Cinema*. Bloomington: Indiana UP, 1984.

de Man, Paul. "Autobiography as De-Facement." *Modern Language Notes* 94 (1979): 919–30.

Deutsch, Helene. *The Psychology of Women*. 2 vols. 1944. New York: Grune, 1965.

Dewar, Hugo. "Grossbritanien." *Die Kommunistischen Parteien der Welt*. Ed. C. D. Kernig. Freiburg: Herder, 1969. 220–27.

Dewey, John. *Art as Experience*. 1934. New York: Paragon, 1979.

Dixon, Marlene. "The Rise of Women's Liberation." *Ramparts* 8.6 (1969): 57–64. Rpt. in *Masculine/Feminine*. Ed. Betty Roszak and Theodore Roszak. New York: Harper, 1969. 186–201.

Doane, Mary Ann, Patricia Mellencamp, and Linda Williams, eds. *Re-Vision: Essays in Feminist Film Criticism*. Frederick: University Publications of America, 1983.

Donovan, Josephine, ed. *Feminist Literary Criticism: Explorations in Theory*. Lexington: UP of Kentucky, 1975.

Draine, Betsy. "Nostalgia and Irony: The Postmodern Order of *The Golden Notebook*." *Modern Fiction Studies* 26 (1980): 31–48. Rpt. in Bertelsen 139–52.

———. *Substance under Pressure: Artistic Coherence and Evolving Form*. Madison: U of Wisconsin P, 1983.

Draper, Theodore. *The Roots of American Communism.* 1957. New York: Viking, 1963.

DuPlessis, Rachel Blau. *Writing beyond the Ending: Narrative Strategies of Twentieth-Century Women Writers.* Bloomington: Indiana UP, 1985.

Edinger, Edward. *Ego and Archetype.* Baltimore: Penguin, 1973.

Elbaz, Robert. "Autobiography, Ideology, and Genre Theory." *Orbis Litterarum* 38 (1983): 187–204.

Eliot, George. *Middlemarch.* Norton Critical Edition. New York: Norton, 1977.

Eliot, T. S. "The Metaphysical Poets." Kermode and Hollander 512–19.

———. "Tradition and the Individual Talent." Kermode and Hollander 505–11.

———. "*Ulysses*, Order and Myth." *Dial* 75 (1923): 480–83. Rpt. in *James Joyce: Two Decades of Criticism.* Ed. Sean Givens. New York: Vanguard, 1948. 198–202.

———. *The Waste Land. Norton Anthology of Modern Poetry.* Ed. Richard Ellmann and Robert O'Claire. New York: Norton, 1973. 457–71.

Ellmann, Mary. *Thinking about Women.* New York: Harcourt, 1968.

Ettinger, S. "The Modern Period." *A History of the Jewish People.* Ed. H. H. Ben-Sasson. Cambridge: Harvard UP, 1976. 727–1096.

Firestone, Shulamith. *The Dialectic of Sex: The Case for a Feminist Revolution.* New York: Morrow, 1970.

Foley, Barbara. "The Modernist Documentary Novel." *Telling the Truth: The Theory and Practice of Documentary Fiction.* Ithaca: Cornell UP, 1986. 185–200.

Freud, Sigmund. *A General Introduction to Psychoanalysis.* 1920. Trans. Joan Riviere. 1924. New York: Pocket, 1975.

Friedan, Betty. *The Feminine Mystique.* New York: Norton, 1963.

———. *The Second Stage.* New York: Summit, 1981.

Fromm, Eric. *Beyond the Chains of Illusion: My Encounter with Marx and Freud.* New York: Simon, 1962.

Gardiner, Judith Kegan. "Gender, Values and Lessing's Cats." *Feminist Issues in Literary Scholarship.* Ed. Shari Benstock. Bloomington: Indiana UP, 1987. 110–23.

Gentile, Mary C. *Film Feminisms: Theory and Practice.* Westport: Greenwood, 1985.

Gilbert, Sandra M., and Susan Gubar. *The Madwoman in the Attic: The Woman Writer and the Nineteenth-Century Literary Imagination.* New Haven: Yale UP, 1979.

Gilbert, Stuart. *James Joyce's Ulysses.* 1930. New York: Vintage, 1955.

Gimlin, Hoyt, ed. *The Women's Movement: Agenda for the '80s.* Washington: Congressional Quarterly, 1981.

Goodman, Ellen. "The Doris Lessing Hoax." Sprague and Tiger 213–14.

Gornick, Vivian. *The Romance of American Communism.* New York: Basic, 1977.

Gornick, Vivian, and Barbara K. Moran, eds. *Woman in Sexist Society: Studies in Power and Powerlessness*. New York: Mentor, 1971.

Gray, Richard. *The Two Nations: Aspects of the Development of Race Relations in the Rhodesias and Nyasaland*. London: Oxford UP, 1960.

Greene, Gayle. "Women and Men in Doris Lessing's *The Golden Notebook*: Divided Selves." *The (M)other Tongue: Essays in Feminist Psychoanalytic Literary Interpretation*. Ed. Shirley Nelson Garner, Claire Kahane, and Madelon Sprengnether. Ithaca: Cornell UP, 1985. 280–305.

Greer, Germaine. *The Female Eunuch*. New York: Bantam, 1971.

Grimm, Reinhold. "Identity and Difference: On Comparative Studies within a Single Language." *Profession 86* (1986): 28–29.

Haight, Gordon S. Introduction. *Middlemarch*. By George Eliot. New York: Houghton, 1956. v–xx.

Hardin, Nancy Shields. "Doris Lessing and the Sufi Way." Pratt and Dembo 148–65.

Harvey, W. J. Introduction. *Middlemarch*. By George Eliot. New York: Penguin, 1965. 7–22.

Hayman, David. *Ulysses: The Mechanics of Meaning*. Rev. ed. Madison: U of Wisconsin P, 1982.

Hedin, Anne. "The Mandala: Blueprint for Change in Lessing's Later Fiction." Bertelsen 163–68.

Hellman, Lillian. *Pentimento: A Book of Portraits*. Boston: Little, 1973.

Hewlett, Sylvia Ann. *A Lesser Life: The Myth of Women's Liberation in America*. New York: Morrow, 1986.

Hinz, Evelyn J., and John J. Teunissen. "The Pieta as Icon in *The Golden Notebook*." *Contemporary Literature* 14 (1973): 457–71. Rpt. in Pratt and Dembo 40–54.

Hite, Molly. "(En)Gendering Metafiction: Women Writers, Experimental Narrative and Doris Lessing's *The Golden Notebook*." Prog. arr. by the Doris Lessing Society, MLA Convention, 28 Dec. 1986.

Hobsbawm, Eric J. *Revolutionaries*. New York: Pantheon, 1973.

Holman, C. Hugh. "The Modernist Period in English Literature." *A Handbook to Literature*. 4th ed. Indianapolis: Bobbs, 1980. 275–76.

Howe, Irving. "Neither Compromise nor Happiness." *New Republic* 15 Dec. 1962: 17–20. Rpt. in Sprague and Tiger 177–81.

Hynes, Joseph. "The Construction of *The Golden Notebook*." *Iowa Review* 4 (1973): 100–13.

Jacobi, Jolande. *Complex/Archetype/Symbol in the Psychology of C. G. Jung*. New York: Bollingen, 1959.

James, C. Vaughan. *Soviet Socialist Realism: Origins and Theory*. New York: St. Martin's, 1973.

Jameson, Fredric. "*Ulysses* in History." McCormack and Stead 126–41.

Johnsen, William A. "Joyce's *Dubliners* and the Futility of Modernism." McCormack and Stead 5–21.

Joyce, James. *A Portrait of the Artist as a Young Man.* 1916. New York: Viking, 1971.

———. Ulysses: *A Critical and Synoptic Edition.* Prepared by Hans Walter Gabler. 3 vols. New York: Garland, 1986.

Jung, C. G. *The Practice of Psychotherapy.* New York: Bollingen, 1954.

———. *Psychological Reflections.* New York: Bollingen, 1970.

Kaplan, Carey, and Ellen Cronan Rose, eds. *Doris Lessing: The Alchemy of Survival.* Athens: Ohio UP, 1988.

Kaplan, Sydney Janet. *Feminine Consciousness in the Modern British Novel.* Urbana: U of Illinois P, 1975.

Kermode, Frank, and John Hollander, eds. *Modern British Literature.* New York: Oxford UP, 1973.

Knapp, Mona. *Doris Lessing.* New York: Ungar, 1984.

Kolakowski, Leszek. *Main Currents of Marxism: Its Rise, Growth and Desolation.* Trans. P. S. Falla. 3 vols. Oxford: Oxford UP, 1981.

Kums, Guido. "Doris Lessing: *The Golden Notebook.*" Fiction: Or, The Language of Our Discontent. Frankfurt: Lang, 1985. 125–87.

Laing, R. D. *The Divided Self: An Existential Study in Sanity and Madness.* 1960. London: Pelican, 1971.

———. *The Politics of Experience.* New York: Pantheon, 1967.

Leavis, F. R. *The Great Tradition.* London: Chatto, 1948.

Legum, Colin, ed. *Africa: A Handbook to the Continent.* Rev. ed. New York: Praeger, 1965.

Lejeune, Philippe. "Autobiography in the Third Person." *New Literary History* 9 (1977): 27–50.

Lessing, Doris. "Autobiography: Impertinent Daughters." *Granta* 14 (1984): 51–68.

———. "Autobiography (Part Two): My Mother's Life." *Granta* 17 (1985): 227–38.

———. *Briefing for a Descent into Hell.* 1971. New York: Vintage, 1981.

———. *The Four-Gated City.* New York: Knopf, 1969.

———. *Going Home.* London: Joseph, 1957.

———. *The Golden Notebook.* 1962. New York: Bantam, 1973.

———. *The Grass Is Singing.* 1950. New York: Ballantine, 1964.

———. Interview. With Catherine Rihoit. *F Magazine* June 1981: 41.

———. "An Interview with Doris Lessing." With Susan Stamberg. *Doris Lessing Newsletter* 8.2 (1984): 3+.

———. "Interview with Doris Lessing." With Heide Ziegler and Christopher Bigsby. *The Radical Imagination and the Liberal Tradition: Interviews with English and American Novelists.* Ed. Ziegler and Bigsby. London: Junction, 1982. 188–208.

———. *Martha Quest*. 1952. New York: NAL, 1970.

———. *The Memoirs of a Survivor*. 1974. New York: Bantam, 1975.

———. *Particularly Cats*. 1967. New York: Panther, 1979.

———. *Prisons We Choose to Live In*. New York: Harper, 1987.

———. *A Small Personal Voice*. Ed. Paul Schlueter. 1974. New York: Vintage, 1975.

———. "The Small Personal Voice." *Declaration*. Ed. Tom Machsler. London: MacGibbon, 1957. 11–27. Rpt. in *A Small Personal Voice* 3–21.

———. "Smart Set Socialists." *New Statesman* 1 Dec. 1961: 822–24.

———. *The Wind Blows Away Our Words*. London: Picador, 1987.

———. "Witness as Prophet." *Time* 25 July 1969: 75.

Levy, Hyman. *Jews and the National Question*. Rev. American ed. New York: Cameron, 1958.

Libby, Marion Vlastos. "Sex and the New Woman in *The Golden Notebook*." *Iowa Review* 5 (1974): 106–20.

Lifson, Martha. "Structural Patterns in *The Golden Notebook*." *Michigan Papers in Women's Studies* 2 (1978): 95–108.

Lightfoot, Marjorie J. "Breakthrough in *The Golden Notebook*." *Studies in the Novel* 7.2 (1975): 277–83.

Lindeman, Albert S. *A History of European Socialism*. New Haven: Yale UP, 1983.

Lindsay, Jack. *After the "Thirties": The Novel in Britain, and Its Future*. London: Lawrence, 1956.

Lodge, David. *The Modes of Modern Writing: Metaphor, Metonymy, and the Typology of Modern Literature*. Ithaca: Cornell UP, 1977.

Loney, Martin. *Rhodesia: White Racism and Imperial Response*. Harmondsworth: Penguin, 1975.

Lukács, Georg. *The Meaning of Contemporary Realism*. Trans. John Mander and Necke Mander. London: Merlin, 1963.

———. "Narrate or Describe?" *Writer and Critic and Other Essays*. New York: Grosset, 1970. 125–43.

Maps on File. New York: Facts on File, 1981

Markow, Alice Bradley. "The Pathology of Feminine Failure in the Fiction of Doris Lessing." *Critique* 16 (1975): 88–100.

Marovitz, Sanford E. "Toward *Moby-Dick*: A Freshman Honors Course." Bickman 56–65.

Mayne, Judith. "The Woman at the Keyhole: Women's Cinema and Feminist Criticism." Doane et al. 49–66.

McCafferey, Larry. *Postmodern Fiction: A Bio-Bibliographical Guide*. New York: Greenwood, 1986.

McCormack, W. J., and Alistair Stead, eds. *James Joyce and Modern Literature*. London: Routledge, 1982.

McDowell, Frederick P. W. "The Fiction of Doris Lessing: An Interim View." *Arizona Quarterly* 21 (1965): 315–45.

Middlemas, Keith. *Power and the Party: Changing Forces of Communism in Western Europe.* London: Deutsch, 1980.

Miller, Hugh. *Introduction to Music.* New York: Barnes, 1958.

Millett, Kate. *Sexual Politics.* 1970. New York: Avon, 1971.

Mills, C. Wright. *The Marxists.* New York: Dell, 1962.

Modleski, Tania. "Rape versus Mans/laughter: Hitchcock's *Blackmail* and Feminist Interpretation." *PMLA* 102 (1987): 304–15.

Morgan, Ellen. "Alienation of the Woman Writer in *The Golden Notebook.*" *Contemporary Literature* 14 (1973): 471–81. Rpt. in Pratt and Dembo 54–63.

Mulkeen, Anne. "Twentieth-Century Realism: The 'Grid' Structure of *The Golden Notebook.*" *Studies in the Novel* 4 (1972): 262–75.

Mulvey, Laura. "Afterthoughts on 'Visual Pleasure and Narrative Cinema' Inspired by *Duel in the Sun.*" *Framework* 15–17 (1981): 12–15.

———. "Changes." *Discourse* 7 (1985): 11–30.

———. "Visual Pleasure and Narrative Cinema." *Screen* 16 (1975): 6–18.

Neumann, Erich. *Depth Psychology and a New Ethic.* 1969. New York: Putnam's, 1973.

Newton, Judith, and Deborah Rosenfelt, eds. *Feminist Criticism and Social Change.* New York: Methuen, 1985.

Oates, Joyce Carol. "A Visit with Doris Lessing." *Southern Review* 9.4 (1973): 873–82.

Olney, James. "Autobiography and the Cultural Moment: A Thematic, Historical, and Bibliographical Introduction." *Autobiography: Essays Theoretical and Critical.* Ed. Olney. Princeton: Princeton UP, 1980. 3–27.

Orwell, George. *Homage to Catalonia.* 1938. New York: Harcourt, 1952.

Ozick, Cynthia. "Women and Creativity: The Demise of the Dancing Dog." *Motive* 29 (1969): 7–16. Rpt. in Gornick and Moran 431–51.

Pascal, Roy. *Design and Truth in Autobiography.* Cambridge: Harvard UP, 1960.

Perrakis, Phyllis Sternberg. "Doris Lessing's *Golden Notebook*: Separation and Symbiosis." *American Imago* 38 (1981): 407–28.

Pratt, Annis. "The Contrary Structure of Doris Lessing's *The Golden Notebook.*" *World Literature Written in English* 12 (1973): 150–61.

Pratt, Annis, and L. S. Dembo, eds. *Doris Lessing: Critical Studies.* Madison: U of Wisconsin P, 1974.

Pratt, Mary Louise. "Comparative Literature as a Cultural Practice." *Profession 86* (1986): 33–35.

Ranger, Terence. *The African Voice in Southern Rhodesia (1898–1930).* London: Heinemann, 1968.

————, ed. *Aspects of Central African History*. London: Heinemann, 1970.

Rapping, Elayne Antler. "Unfree Women: Feminism in Doris Lessing's Novels." *Women's Studies* 3 (1975): 29–44.

Raskin, Jonah. "Doris Lessing at Stony Brook." [Interview.] Lessing, *A Small Personal Voice* 61–76.

Ray, J. Karen. "The Ethics of Feminism in the Literature Classroom: A Delicate Balance." *English Journal* 74 (1985): 54–59.

Register, Cheri. "American Feminist Literary Criticism: A Bibliographical Introduction." Donovan 1–28.

Renza, Louis A. "The Veto of the Imagination: A Theory of Autobiography." *New Literary History* 9 (1977): 1–26.

Rose, Ellen Cronan. "Doris Lessing: The International Response: Commentary." Prog. arr. by the Doris Lessing Society, MLA Convention, 29 Dec. 1986.

Rubenstein, Roberta. "Briefing on Inner Space: Doris Lessing and R. D. Laing." *Psychoanalytic Review* 63 (1976): 83–95.

————. "Doris Lessing's *The Golden Notebook*: The Meaning of Its Shape." *American Imago* 31 (1975): 40–58.

————. *The Novelistic Vision of Doris Lessing: Breaking the Forms of Consciousness*. Urbana: U of Illinois P, 1979.

Russ, Joanna. *How to Suppress Women's Writing*. Austin: U of Texas P, 1983.

Russian Institute, eds. *The Anti-Stalin Campaign and International Communism: A Selection of Documents*. New York: Columbia UP, 1956.

Sartre, Jean-Paul. *The Specter of Stalin*. Trans. Irene Clepane. London: Hamilton, 1965.

————. *What Is Literature?* 1947. Trans. Bernard Frechtman. 1949. New York: Washington Square, 1966.

Schweickart, Patrocinio P. "Reading a Wordless Statement: The Structure of Doris Lessing's *The Golden Notebook*." *Modern Fiction Studies* 31 (1985): 263–79.

Sedgwick, Peter. *Psycho Politics*. New York: Harper, 1982.

Seligman, Dee. *Doris Lessing: An Annotated Bibliography of Criticism*. Westport: Greenwood, 1981.

————. "The Four-Faced Novelist." *Modern Fiction Studies* 26 (1980): 3–16.

————. "The Sufi Quest." *World Literature Written in English* 12 (1973): 190–207.

Showalter, Elaine. *A Literature of Their Own: British Women Novelists from Brontë to Lessing*. Princeton: Princeton UP, 1977.

————, ed. *The New Feminist Criticism: Essays on Women, Literature and Theory*. New York: Pantheon, 1985.

————. "Women Writers and the Double Standard." Gornick and Moran 452–79.

Sigal, Clancy. *Going Away*. Boston: Houghton, 1962.

————. *Zone of the Interior*. New York: Crowell, 1976.

Singleton, Mary Ann. *The City and the Veld: The Fiction of Doris Lessing*. Lewisburg: Bucknell UP, 1977.

Sked, Alan, and Chris Cook. *Post-War Britain: A Political History*. Harmondsworth: Penguin, 1979.

Sontag, Susan. *On Photography*. New York: Farrar, 1977.

Spacks, Patricia Meyer. *The Female Imagination*. New York: Knopf, 1975.

———. "Free Women." *Hudson Review* 24 (1971–72): 559–73.

Spencer, Sharon. "Femininity and the Woman Writer: Doris Lessing's *The Golden Notebook* and the *Diary* of Anaïs Nin." *Women's Studies* 1 (1973): 180–89.

Spilka, Mark. "Lessing and Lawrence: The Battle of the Sexes." *Contemporary Literature* 16 (1975): 218–240. Rpt. in Sprague and Tiger 69–86.

Sprague, Claire. "Doris Lessing's *Reasoner* Letters." *Doris Lessing Newsletter* 3.1 (1979): 6–8.

———. *Rereading Doris Lessing: Narrative Patterns of Doubling and Repetition*. Chapel Hill: U of North Carolina P, 1987.

Sprague, Claire, and Virginia Tiger, eds. *Critical Essays on Doris Lessing*. Boston: Hall, 1986.

Spriano, Paolo. *Stalin and the European Communists*. Trans. Jon Rothschild. London: Verso, 1985.

Steele, Murray. "Doris Lessing's Rhodesia." Bertelsen 44–54.

———. "White Working Class Disunity: The Southern Rhodesia Labour Party." *Rhodesian History* 1 (1970): 59–81.

Stelzig, Eugene L. "Poetry and/or Truth: An Essay on the Confessional Imagination." *University of Toronto Quarterly* 54 (1984): 17–37.

Stitzel, Judith. "Reading Doris Lessing." *College English* 40 (1979): 498–504.

Sturrock, John. "The New Model Autobiographer." *New Literary History* 9 (1977): 51–62.

Sukenick, Lynn. "Feeling and Reason in Doris Lessing's Fiction." *Contemporary Literature* 14 (1973): 515–35. Rpt. in Pratt and Dembo 98–118.

Sultan, Stanley. *The Argument of* Ulysses. Columbus: Ohio State UP, 1964.

Sworakowski, Witold. *World Communism: A Handbook*. Stanford: Hoover Institution, 1973.

Taylor, Jenny. "Memory and Desire on Going Home: The Deconstruction of a Colonial Radical." Bertelsen 55–63.

———, ed. *Notebooks/Memoirs/Archives: Reading and Rereading Doris Lessing*. Boston: Routledge, 1982.

Thomson, Boris. *Lot's Wife and the Venus of Milo: Conflicting Attitudes to the Cultural Heritage in Modern Russia*. London: Cambridge UP, 1978.

Tovey, Donald Francis. *The Forms of Music*. New York: Meridian, 1956.

Trotsky, Leon. *Literature and Revolution*. 1923. Trans. Rose Trunsky. 1960. Ann Arbor: U of Michigan P, 1971.

Vambe, Lawrence. *An Ill-Fated People: Rhodesia before and after Rhodes*. London: Heinemann, 1972.

Vlastos, Marion. "Doris Lessing and R. D. Laing: Psychopolitics and Prophecy." *PMLA* 91 (1976): 245–57. Rpt. in Sprague and Tiger 126–41.

Waugh, Patricia. *Metafiction: The Theory and Practice of Self-Conscious Fiction*. London: Methuen, 1984.

Webb, Marilyn. "Becoming the Men We Wanted to Marry: Feminism and Doris Lessing." *Village Voice* 4 Jan. 1973: 1.

Weinrich, A. K. H. *Black and White Elites in Rural Rhodesia*. Manchester: Manchester UP, 1973.

Williams, Linda. "When the Woman Looks." Doane et al. 83–99.

Williams, Raymond. *The Long Revolution*. 1961. Westport: Greenwood, 1975.

Wilson, Sharon R. "Camera Images in Margaret Atwood's Novels." *Margaret Atwood: Reflections and Reality*. Ed. Beatrice Mendez-Egle. Edinburg: Pan American UP, 1987. 29–57.

Wood, Neal. *Communism and British Intellectuals*. New York: Columbia UP, 1959.

Woolf, Virginia. "Mr. Bennett and Mrs. Brown." *Collected Essays*. 4 vols. London: Hogarth, 1966–67. 1: 319–37.

———. *A Room of One's Own*. 1929. New York: Harcourt, 1957.

Yardley, Jonathan. "Lessing Is More: An 'Unknown' Author and the Success Syndrome." Sprague and Tiger 215–17.

INDEX

DATE D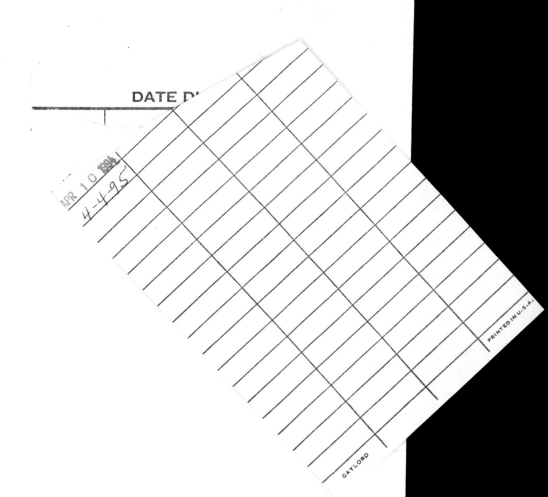

APR 10 1994

4-4-95

PRINTED IN U.S.A.

GAYLORD